Rhubarbs From a Rock

Rhubarbs From a Rock

(Escaping the Rat Race)

David Fagan

iUniverse, Inc.
New York Lincoln Shanghai

Rhubarbs From a Rock
(Escaping the Rat Race)

iUniverse, Inc.

For information address:
iUniverse, Inc.
2021 Pine Lake Road, Suite 100
Lincoln, NE 68512
www.iuniverse.com

ISBN: 0-595-30246-7

Printed in the United States of America

With Thanks

Dedicated with gratitude to my adopted neighbourhood, the citizens of Hydra, whose shenanigans have supplied me with an endless list of fond memories.

In particular for the prodding from William Pownall and Francesca Meks Taylor, Charlotte Gusay and Barbara Lapček who gave me the impetus to persevere.

And specifically for the support, friendship and sustenance of Maggie Martin, who was always there through thick and thin.

This book wouldn't have seen the light of day, without Kelsey the rock at my side, to whom I wish the cosmos.

Contents

Pigeon Holes

What makes a bloke give up a promising career in advertising and move to a Greek island thirty years premature to normal retirement date? Trading golf clubs for fishing line; two cars and life insurance, for sandals and hand-to-mouth. I have masticated over this ad-nauseam, eventually putting it down to fate—and one lunch in 1983.

I am a gent who doesn't know which Zodiac sign goes when, unless it's mentioned with a specific date that's annually repetitive. I wouldn't call myself a fatalist but how I came to live for nearly two decades on Hydra Island, Greece, a "Rock" in the Saronic Gulf, was decidedly fortuitous.

It was my first visit to Greece and my travelling companion was in the driving seat. We "package coached" it on our first day to Delphi. Our busload of cameras were politely shepherded around ruins and oracles by a shrill guide. Time schedules were kept.

We scheduled ourselves down the coastline in another tour bus to visit the spectacular ruins at Sounion the next day. We also visited ancient ruins around the Plaka that night. I mentioned to my then girlfriend, that I hoped our itinerary included some beaches and islands, less tramping and more basking.

She returned to the hotel room from the info office with tickets to the islands pencilled in for the following morning. A coach was picking us up at 7.00 am to ferry us to the port she explained.

Shortly after dawn I was packing.

"What are you doing? We're coming back tonight; just take a towel and swimming costume for the beach."

The "island-hopping package" included three islands in one day, "back before dark" the receipt had announced.

Aegina was delightful; I photographed a temple and a huge, brightly coloured Cadillac that was barely able to squeeze down an alley. We reboarded the cruise ship an hour later.

At Poros, a dog caught the ship's rope and the mixed bag of tourists bundled off to investigate the quay-front shops and photograph fishing ciaquis. Everyone re-embarked on schedule.

It was siesta time when we landed for our allotted sixty minutes on Hydra. Little did I guess it was to become home for half my life. Ironically it was to be this beach-less rock that magnetised me. One that is also vehicle-less; mules languish in a corner of the harbour, not a moped in hearing nor a bicycle in sight.

It was postcard picturesque, population two and a half thousand according the guide pamphlet. There was a sense of it being timeless, tranquillity oozed out of whitewashed walls and cobbled streets, an apparent paradise.

We didn't get back on the cruise ship.

Compulsion to investigate the island further found me negotiating the price for a pension room at the back of the port. Next I called our hotel in Athens who obligingly agreed to pack our belongings and store our suitcases until we were "un-marooned"; there were island shops that sold basic toiletries etc.

That evening I saw a sign, which rang a bell. "Bill's Bar", a place I had heard mentioned by a fellow I worked with who had been to Greece.

It was just opening when I asked for Bill.

"Anyone here know Bill?" echoed a loud retort in surprisingly eloquent English the gent fidgeting behind the counter asked a pair of early regulars who looked like part of the furniture.

"Give the boy a drink," they ragged, inviting me over to their table once the owner had poured me a "large one". I found myself joining the fixtures in their corner for most of the evening, which led to a lunch invitation the following day.

We putt-putted our way down the coast in a small ciaqui to a house only accessible by rickety wooden jetty and had lunch over-looking the Saronic Gulf. Twelve different nationalities amongst sixteen guests; conversation was sparkling and varied. It was the melting pot of my dreams set upon one of the most picturesque of Mediterranean islands.

Several courses ambulated out, which led to further sundowners and further rendezvous. Without traffic life slows down, not a wheel to be seen, the fastest thing one saw in the port was a scampering cat.

The setting and community were intoxicating and I decided to stay as long as I could. The hook was set.

Two decades on I am still "marooned".

"So what do you do?" is not a popular line opener on the island.

It's just not the done thing; people come here to get away from what they do.

It's a question that I still have difficulty answering—whilst living on the Rock I have incorporated all manner of island industry.

I even have trouble pigeon holing myself when it comes to background. Irish, African and Greek influences have shaped my outlook and my "inlook"; in short I cheer for a lot of countries during world cups.

Anthony Kingsmill, legendary on the island as a laureate and artist, once succinctly advised me, "as long as you justify your existence old bean."

I took heed and have resorted to all manner of activities over the years to justify my existence. Donkeys have become as much a part of my life as cars are to city-folk.

Having committed myself to a partnership in a bar and restaurant, I returned to Africa to flog my belongings, quit my job and generally liquidate my life in the rat race. I returned permanently to Hydra in '85 to live my "dream come true", but as it turned out, it was nothing like my wildest dreams.

I quickly learned, within a year of the bar opening, that there is nothing simple about island living. I found myself confronted with potentially four years in the Greek courts in order to keep it alive because I had failed to read the small print.

So I abandoned inn keeping and opted for simpler, less complicated forms of graft. But even that wasn't straightforward; complication is the name of the game living this "simple" island life.

Over the last twenty years, I have been granted the opportunity to meet some wonderful people who have had an influence on my life, in circumstances and places that I could only have imagined if I'd stayed behind an office desk.

I am genuinely surprised by people who tell me they think it was brave to give up a secure life and dwell fulltime on a Greek island; I happen to regard facing ten traffic jams a week as courageous.

The island has acquired the nickname of the "Rock" not just because of its obvious geographical depiction, but similarities to Alcatraz in its captivation power. The Eagles song "you can check out, but you can never leave" is a simile often quoted by its inmates.

These snippets of life on a Rock are my random "rhubarbs" about some aspects of an alternative way of life from one inmate's point of view.

The word *rhubarb* has crept into my vocabulary as an expression for the shenanigans that accompany any activity on the island. Two or three individuals standing around a live microphone in a radio theatre "rhubarbing", gives the audio impression of a debating mob. Nothing on Hydra seems to happen without a rhubarb, not even changing a light bulb.

Dim and Dimmer

I remember thinking that he was going to electrocute himself and that I should say something. But then I figured he was the qualified technician and I was new to the island. Everything was new to me, including the fact that electrical wiring was supposed to look like spaghetti; bare un-connected wires protruding from weird places were normal.

I let him throw the switch—

It was the morning before the re-opening night of my bar and Yanni had finally turned up, small donkey laden with toolboxes and coils of wire.

"I came before but they were painting." His explanation for the three-week delay.

I'd thought the idea of using a dimmer switch for the lights over the bar would be a simple affair. A switch with a knob, that swiveled, allowing one to set the mood. Seemed like a grand idea, the final touch to the refurbishments.

I pointed to the light switch behind the bar.

"Yes, I have, very good, German model," he enthused.

Trouble was the German model didn't fit in the hole and a pneumatic drill plus some hammers were unloaded.

Behind the beam above the little bar it looked like a flex highway; some so old and corroded they were black, others in various shades of brown depending on which decade they'd been tacked. None of the old wiring appeared live, so more cable was brought off the donkey.

I watched Yanni put a clean white cord over the top of the old electrics, tap tapping nails indiscriminately. A small hint of the pyrotechnics to follow.

It looked grand. I was impressed with how Yanni had managed to work out the wiring and get the dimmer device flush. And I still had time to clean up the debris.

"Top job," he exclaimed triumphantly and turned the knob.

For a second I thought I heard oil boiling in the kitchen until I noticed the blue and green sparks fizzling up the wall in front of Yanni's nose.

There was a loud bang, some bottles fell over and we were left standing in the gloom. Yanni's silhouette had perpendicular hair.

Immediate concern overwhelmed the urge to burst out laughing.

"Yanni, you okay?"

"There was a fault with the switch," he appeared more disturbed by the product's flaw. "I will get another."

I could only assume he was used to tests failing and had the heart of an ox.

Two hours later he returned. I had swept the rubble and cleaned the black scorch marks from the fresh paint as best I could.

"The German's is kaput, but I have Italian switch, very good," he said, brandishing a different dimmer. "Ees second hand, but ees very strong."

Some more adjusting to the hole size occurred.

This time it appeared to work. We turned the wattage down and then up.

"Top job," said Yanni, in a satisfied voice turning to go.

There was a pop and tinkle of light glass on the counter, followed by another explosion in the wall. Gloom and silence.

"Well Yanni?"

A hesitation before he replied, "I will put the old switch back and make that work until I can order a Japanese switch."

I expressed my disappointment, suspecting this could mean weeks of delay.

"No worries, we fix it all today," he assured me.

He replaced the original on/off switch, taping it into the now enlarged hole so it didn't wobble.

It worked; at least I would have lighting on re-opening night, albeit too bright.

"We will have dimmer, don't worry." He grabbed a tea towel and unscrewed a middle light bulb.

"And if you want dimmer," he proceeded to unscrew a second. "You see everything works out in the end."

Top job indeed!

Colour Blind

"You paint the bar, it smells fresh?" asked Pavlos, settling onto his usual stool. "Good to have it open again, we missed you."

He was my first customer, regular as clockwork, same stool, same drink and same game every night except Sundays.

Pavlos spoke some English having served in the Greek merchant navy for years. He had been forced into early retirement by an illness, which had left him almost totally blind so knew the island by brail.

He was keen to start poker dice as was our ritual. We would play whilst I polished glasses.

"Penta asses," my first toss on re-opening night.

Five aces! Against a blind man; and no witnesses, a mixed omen?

"Penta asses?" was all he repeated mildly before he threw his dice. I remember wishing he would throw five aces too that night so I could reciprocate the call.

I had purchased the bar at the end of the previous "season" and had decided to keep it open over the winter while I settled into island life.

It had been a marvellous opportunity to get to know the inhabitants and cut my teeth in the bar business before my first full summer.

My "Bahia Bar" became a local clubhouse. These were the days before televisions invaded the island. Expats and locals would play chess, *tavli* (backgammon), cards, dice, dominoes and even break out charades. Spontaneous guitars would periodically motivate parties.

Muleteers and fishermen would bundle in and order in quantities, sometimes taking a whole bottle of spirit to their table. The islanders were most convivial. "*Yassou*" (hello) or "*kalispera*" (good evening), I would reply as they trickled in. Pleasant noises to a new innkeepers ear.

The bar was small but had a couple of unique features, a two-hundred-year-old oven and an open *cisterna* (water well). Apart from the fresh appearance and novel wiring, I'd thought that I'd come up with a great idea during the refurbishments to resolve a rhubarb surrounding the cisterna opening. I was keen to see the reaction.

The problem with the cisterna had been that when the little bar filled up, or when one's customers had consumed gill limits of alcohol, it would be used as an ashtray, indeed ashtrays themselves were known to fall in. Some more sensitive noses had lobbied for its closure. Health concerns had been voiced too.

"Lord knows what's fermenting down there," a Swiss nose had twitched.

Another bunch said that the cisterna wellhead, situated almost bang in the middle of the room, was what made the place and gave it unique character. To touch it would be sacrilege. Also, said others, one couldn't alter any building more than two centuries old by law. One had to work within the existing architecture, or submit plans to the Department of Ecological Affairs for approval; a time consuming procedure said to involve brown envelopes if one wanted expedience.

One winter's evening prior to my ingenious refurbishment, a New York banker's pair of spectacles fell down the hole with a splash. Flashlights reflected off the black water about four meters down. Cobwebs laced the tunnelled rock face below broom level. It required a brave and nimble man to enter the hole.

A runner was sent with a message for Pan at his bar. He promised to come by after work. Pan a Vietnam veteran, looked like a slightly stunted, hairy biker from the hard rock era.

He upheld the reputation of being the island's "Rambo". No-Nonsense-Pan was hailed whenever there was trouble.

Short and stocky, with impressive beard and mane, he barely squeezed into the circumference.

"Pan, I'll be forever in your debt," said the Bank, squinting at the disappearing mop.

"There's fuggin' a lot of shit down here,"—some splashing and grunting. A cobweb-beard emerged, glasses clenched in his teeth.

"*Efharisto para poli Pan*," from the grateful Bank holding out his hand.

"5,000 Drachmas," a palm went out.

"But a new pair only costs 2,000," blurted Wall Street, when confronted with a price tag for the service. Financial negotiations and basic economics were second nature to the bloke.

"Then go to Athens to buy some, you know whaddimean," said Pan, not budging an inch.

"Okay, 3,000 and that's extremely generous," countered the Bank.

"Lions, tigers, sharks okay, but fuggin' spiders—*oxi* (no)," retorted Pan, making a point of brushing out the beard. "I risk my life so you can see—Okay 5,500 Drachmas."

"4,000!" Brave that banker.

"6,000," haggled the Beard, with a glance to the proprietor. "It's dangerous, you know whaddimean?"

There was a prolonged pause while this transaction was mentally processed. Things were not going Wall Street's way; the cost of a trip to Athens and hours wasted, carried the day—just.

"Done," grumbled the Bank.

It was this incident that sparked the idea, which I'd thought was a decent compromise for all arguments and would also be beneficial to Hydra's wild life, the cats.

During the renovations, I'd blocked the cisterna off inside the wellhead at ground level and made it watertight. Then I'd installed a small kitchen plug so it could be drained and cleaned.

Just before Pavlos came in on the re-opening night, I had filled it with a few inches of water and thrown in a few coins. A wishing well for the cats of Hydra!

Apart from Pavlos, the other locals tended to come later, the expats arriving first. Some threw a couple of coins in for luck and complimented me on the choice of colour scheme.

Françoise, a Parisian fashion designer and animal lover, went straight over to the well for a look. "Zees is a good idea," she said, throwing in a five-hundred-drachma note.

When the first moustache arrived, the usual jovial banter was missing. He peered disapprovingly into the well.

"*Tea-naf-toe*," (what is this) he asked, twisting his right hand with a little shake of his head, indicating non-comprehension.

"For the cats," I said, showing him the little sign I had made saying so in both Greek and English.

He shrugged, sat down and didn't want anything to drink, miming that he was waiting for his mates. Not a comment about the new décor.

Perhaps I had broken protocol by sealing the cisterna, so Pavlos asked him what he thought about the wishing-well idea for me. The moustache said he thought I was a little crazy, but sealed or not, it was of no concern to him. A couple of his mates turned up and their response was similar, or perhaps I should say no response. The wishing well was ignored.

Pavlos sensed the disapproval and suddenly asked me, "What colour you paint the bar?"

"White with green trimming."

"Why?"

I explained that green is Irish and that it happened to be my favourite colour.

"Ahhh—so you no passock?"

I couldn't figure out what he was trying to say.

"What's that?"

"PASOK, a socialist, this island is mostly Nea Democratic—blue and white."

"And green, I take it, is the opposition?"

"Yes PASOK, the socialists."

Pavlos informed the bunch huddled in the corner that I had no political stance and that green was for Irish luck.

"*Ahh Eirlandos,*" followed with guffaws, thumps on backs and drinks all round.

With that Captain Jani, who was often called the island mascot, came in and worked up quite a fuss about the sealed off cisterna.

Jani had disabilities; coherent speech was one of them, but the animations clarified his point.

"*Oxi!*" on the cisterna job.

Everyone loved Jani; he fished for the cats and caught boat ropes for cigars. He never accepted money unless he could reciprocate by buying one's newspaper and such. Jani had much pride, many morals and nothing on his feet.

It was explained to Jani, that the well was to make a good-luck wish and that the change would go towards feeding the cats.

At this his face lit up, he gave me a smelly hug, rolled up his jumper sleeve and took all the cash, including Françoise's five-hundred drying with a peg on the metal arch above the well.

"What's he doing?" I asked Pavlos.

"He is going to buy food for the cats with it," he explained.

"*Bravo rai Jani,*" I encouraged. "*Etsi,*" echoed the moustaches in the corner.

Jani would regularly empty the well on his way out thereafter.

Anthony, a permanent member, would saunter in every night to holler down "are you well?" He would chuckle to himself at this silly joke. "I see Jani's been at you again," before sideling up to the bar.

His chilled glass of house wine would be waiting in front of a stool, adjacent to wherever the poker game had progressed to.

"Beat me to it," he would say, winking in jest. "It was supposed to buy me into a round of dice."

I know some cats did well for a while too.

Dogs, Donkeys & Do-Gooders

Territorial disputes, especially in a small community, tend to get up close and personal.

Mike didn't like the look of me and there was nothing I could do about it. He was simply a bully. The more I encountered him, the more our mutual dislike intensified and ours is a little island so avoidance was almost impossible. He made me nervous and he knew it.

His self-proclaimed territory included monopolizing the local supermarket entrance; the closest alternative shop was a good walk downhill to the port. The trouble with Mike was his unpredictability. Most of the time he would lounge passively in the sun, but every now and again he would feel the need to get upright and macho. One ran a daily mental gauntlet; either risk Mike's mood at the local shop, or take the hike.

Mike was a mean dog; black as his mood and built like a Mastiff. His gene pool probably included every known form of large canine breed in the Med.

Even basking in the Saronic sun, he would grumble and hoist half an upper lip to show you his ivory just in case you might have forgotten whose turf you were on. It was only a matter of time before some incident occurred and when it did, the ensuing riot was amazing.

Mike's imposed no-walk-zone was about a hundred meters either side of a scruffy little shack situated just off, what is affectionately known by expats as Donkey Shit Lane, the main route from Hydra Town to Kamini. The inhabitants of the shack were the many offspring of a local fisherman and his large unkempt wife, who appeared to produce an additional family member every year. They earned the nickname of the "Bare-Foot-Tribe", an uncouth mob that haunted Mike's domain and did nothing to discourage his inhospitable disposition.

Most of the time I took my chances and prayed I'd escape the dog's wrath, rather than walk the long route home.

I'd had a bad day; the third consecutive spent in fruitless waiting for an illusive plumber and there were no supplies at home. When Mike started rumbling his disapproval at my intrusion into his district I flicked my cigarette end with reflex annoyance in his general direction.

Perhaps Mike thought it was a peace offering, some tasty morsel. Whatever his motive, I watched in fascination as he gave a little jump with his front paws and deftly caught the glowing ember in the back of his throat. His jaws snapped shut like a rattrap. I suppose if he had swallowed a nest of hornets the result might have been the same.

Mike went nuts and I, the perpetrator of his discomfort, was still standing right in front of him. Extraordinary sounds issued forth as he launched himself at me. Instinctively I whacked the animal upon the side of his ear-flattened head with my leather shoulder bag in self-defence.

My bag was a rather clumsy saddlebag affair, which I always lugged about with me. It contained the vestiges of my life: outdated filofax, cigs, lighter, wallet, bunches of keys, my lucky Chinese musical ball, a Swiss army knife, some fishing tackle plus few screws and nails for emergencies. The contents were all loosely covered by a flap, which because of constant use and the lack of pick pockets on the island, was never buckled shut.

The bag exploded on impact, raining noise on the cobblestones, which in turn attracted the attention of the Bare-Foot-Tribe who emerged from their dwelling to see what all the commotion was about. The enraged Mike, emboldened by the arrival of reinforcements, redoubled his efforts at trying to extinguish his smouldering tonsils on some soft, cool part of my anatomy.

I was too shocked by this sudden turn of events to act rationally so added to the cacophony by yelling incoherently at the dog.

It was at this particular instant that a donkey-train hove into view around a corner.

The lead animal was laden with plastic rubbish-bags stuffed into two large baskets, on either side of its wooden saddle. It was having none of this excitement and turned to escape. In its haste to flee, it caught the plastic liners on a nail sticking out of the wall spewing trash onto the street.

The muleteer had obviously also been the brunt of Mike's disfavour in the past and came to my rescue. Wielding a large stick he entered the fray with enthusiasm and a yell, his donkeys braying for back up.

Then the owner of an adjacent house, a quiet, retired expatriate who valued his serene surroundings, put in an appearance. He already had an ongoing feud with the unruly "Shoeless Clan" about their constant littering and lack of discipline. The developing scene on his doorstep obviously merited some law enforcement. It was suspected that it was he who summoned the local constabulary.

In the meantime the size of this animated debate grew, neighbourhood *Yayas* (grandmothers), another dog and some builders got involved. Even *Keeria* (Mrs.) Maria, elephantiasis and stick-wielding terrorizer of children, managed to waddle up with an important vocal point of view.

The sight of two uniformed police did nothing to dampen the spirit of the occasion. Indeed their arrival seemed to encourage more chaos, with all the contenders voicing their version of the story. Each was convinced that he who shouted loudest and gesticulated the most, would get heard first and therefore have the sympathetic ear of the law. And would thus, the primary concern, not be held accountable for cleaning up the now trampled mess.

The smaller cop, newly posted to the island, decided to settle the matter and laid down the law; the offending dog was henceforth to be tied up.

That should have been the end of it, but the unfortunate policeman didn't know the can of judicial worms that he was opening with this declaration. The Bare-Foot-Tribe were already convicted offenders for tying up their animals. And now they were being ordered to re-tie their dog?

They had previously owned an enormous Great Dane cross breed, which they had dutifully tied up because it too, had acquired the habit of terrorizing passers by. Local pedestrians and tourists alike had complained, so a restraining order had been placed on the family hound.

The trouble was they'd gone to the other extreme. This animal had been tied up with a two-foot rope and left to roast in the summer sun, often without water. An unhappy specimen to behold!

A flamboyant Austrian Countess and part-time island resident, had taken pity on its predicament and had gone to the local law about the family's cruelty to animals. She was also known for going shoeless, the difference being her toenails were brightly manicured and ornaments dangled from a chain around her ankle.

It had been ruled that the fisherman's tribe must not tie up their pet in future, of course leaving it to pursue its original persecution of passer's by. This particular quandary had been resolved by her "Barefootness'" adoption of said huge dog. She eventually took it with her, back to her schloss and large estate, where it could chase rabbits to its heart's content.

The unsuspecting policeman, unaware of the previous events and history, was ungraciously informed of the ruling and told that if he wanted to change the existing corpus juris, then they wanted to see a court order stating so; signed by the Minister of Domestic Affairs himself as well!

The incident had now been elevated to the status of judicial hearings and future court dates. As the instigator of this situation, would I be prepared to mobilize a team of legal troops to take this matter further, the smaller cop enquired of me.

The entire affair had now been placed in my innocent pedestrian lap.

I declined taking official action. Shopping downtown was by far the cheaper and easier option—I would get word when Mike was eventually moved or manacled.

A Various Selection of Shortcuts

An exhausted hiker once described a gentle walk in the country with Jeanette, as a route march and forage expedition.

The word "shortcut" once employed, is never to be trusted again. Jeanette's interpretation of the word involved thorns, stings, wildlife and life threatening heights.

She herself appears impervious to pain, regularly grasping clusters of stinging nettles en-route and stuffing them into a bag for *mezes* (snacks).

She had come to live in Greece as a young woman and had spent her life accumulating rural survival tactics. One couldn't doubt the exotic taste of her nettle soup, purple *loulouthis* (flower) pâté or wild asparagus dishes. Multi-lingual and with a talent for project management, she was held in high regard by the locals having worked with and among them for over three decades.

"I need a hand on my next trip to Othonis," Jeanette offered.

I hadn't heard of the place and asked for details.

"A small island, half the size of Hydra, situated between Greece, Albania and Italy. Under a hundred inhabitants; census age would be about sixty-five and no one speaks English," she enthused. "Untouched, very lush, wonderful diving and great fishing."

Having grown up in Africa, this sounded like it had the makings of a decent safari so I grabbed the opportunity.

Little did I know that the Othonis outing would rival any African adventure.

"Martienne will pick us up in Piraeus and we'll drive to Patras over the Corinth Canal with her." Jeanette had the whole trip planned. "We'll catch the night ferry to Corfu and stay in the Astron Hotel—it's run by friends of mine who won't mind us getting in very late."

"In the morning after breakfast we can take a scenic drive up to the north-ern port of Corfu and catch a fishing ciaqui to Othonis," Jeanette continued. "We should get into port before it gets dark and the pony can take us up the hill. Home for sunset!"

Sounded idyllic—and organised.

"Leon is going to have to come with us." A suitable dog sitter could not be found apparently. "So he'll have to share the back seat."

I had no problem with that. I had a soft spot for the old guy. We had shared food and fire together the previous winter when I'd been house sitting while Jeanette was on a trip to the UK. We knew each other well. Leon was then, probably a hundred and twenty-five in doggie years and suffered from memory loss. Jeanette had called us to see how we were doing. "And how's the old man?" I was on the phone downstairs but had heard the click-click of Leon's long toenails on the wooden floor above me.

"We're both fine, sitting in front of the fire upstairs, watching videos," I replied.

Staying in Jeanette's house was a luxury. A cupboard full of videos to watch on an island with no cinema and almost non-existent television, next to an open log fire. It was decadence.

While we were talking, Leon had stopped directly above me and paused.

"I'm becoming a cordon-blue at spaghetti bolognaise," I said, cheerfully.

Jeanette had left ample mince and pasta in the house for us to eat.

"How's Blighty—" I'd started to enquire before I'd realized what the small drilling sound above me was but by then it was too late. Leon had ambled over to cock his leg against the grand piano and it had gone straight through a crack in the floorboards.

"Swine dog," I'd squawked into Jeanette ear. She'd roared.

So I was well acquainted with Leon and had some idea of what travelling with him would be like.

The safari assembled. Leon, Martienne, Jeanette, a chain saw and myself managed to squeeze in between the luggage. What Martienne lacked in city driving skills, having had two minor incidents trying to find her way out of congested traffic, she made up for in speed on the open road.

Martienne was French and did not like being passed apparently.

"An Alfa Romeo can't beat my Golf," exclaimed the Gallic art dealer, dis-playing surprising enthusiasm for motorized competition as she put her foot down. Superior horses and a hair-raising over-take on a bend put us back in the lead shortly before we reached the Canal.

Then the "Designer Stubble" in the red Alfa took up the challenge and reclaimed the lead minutes later. A gentle scenic drive through the country had become a matter of death-defying speed and defending honour.

My fear during the "race" was probably even more accentuated by the fact that it was my first car ride in many moons. After prolonged periods on the Rock, it takes a little time to get used to traffic. As a pedestrian on Hydra one never moves faster than at a brisk walk. Even motorbikes seem like warp-drive for a while.

I enquired as to the existence of speed traps—a hopeful hint.

"Oui, but zay never uze zem ziss time." The right foot remained flat.

Needless to say, Martienne put us on the ferry at Patras well ahead of schedule. The old dog and I hadn't leaked much and I think we beat the Alfa.

The next day, by the time we had scoured Corfu's market for "basic necessities" and got to Sidari on the northern tip of the island, it was early afternoon. Our accumulated luggage looked like the trappings for a farmhouse.

The ciaqui turned out to be a sixteen-foot fishing boat. Dog, plants, bags and a various selection of forest clearing equipment, were loaded on to the deck.

"About four or five hours—if the weather's okay," announced the fisherman.

It wasn't.

Our sunset was made spectacular by the presence of cloud and escalating winds gave it movement. Leon was getting seasick and tacking into waves became necessary.

Soon after dark, a speck of light on the horizon beckoned but it was another hour before we carefully navigated our way through the reef to the quay.

The pony revealed itself to be of the four-wheeled Citroen variety; I was grateful. Jeanette knew that joke worked in her favour and chuckled while we loaded.

"*To batteria pethanie,*" a helpful moustache informed us, when we tried to start the dust-covered jeep.

"How long since she was driven?" I asked.

"Months, but not to worry there are a couple of other vehicles on the island—mainly tractors—but someone's bound to have jump leads."

The town of Othonis consisted of a dozen buildings and a church. Two tavernas were the hub. One doubled as the post office and magistrates court, the other as a supermarket. The rest of the island's inhabitants were scattered on farms.

Jump leads took time and a lot of walking.

"It's lobster season," said Jeanette. "Let's get up before sunrise and lay some traps—I've got a boat and a new outboard."

Leaving Leon behind the next morning, we marched for ten minutes by flashlight, through the bush to where the pony was parked on the peninsula road. This in reality was a dirt track running through the centre of the hilly island, connecting the town to the island's northern attraction, the lighthouse.

Fog rolled in as we headed down the mountain in twilight.

"Only a bit of morning mist, it'll evaporate when the sun comes up," said Jeanette glibly, when she caught my glance.

Our vessel wasn't much bigger than a suitcase, but the motor was brand new and I optimistically put my faith in the skipper.

"Pass me the instruction book behind you," she said, as we wobbled in the middle of the small harbour. "How does one start these things?"

It should have been a clue.

We managed to thread our way out of the reef with me peering in the gloom for marker beacons. The sea carried swell, but was a smooth as glass, tranquil but eerie.

We motored out to sea. The mist got slightly brighter but wasn't showing signs of thinning as time went by. Skiers call it snow blindness.

"Jeanette do you have a compass?"

"We don't need one, I know exactly where we are," she answered with confidence. "Just start looking for fisherman buoys, we must be getting close to the catchment area."

It was difficult to guess knots or direction when surrounded by a light grey blanket, but I judged the captain to have maintained a steady hand on the tiller. Meaning that we could have been miles out to sea in a bathtub without a compass—in a fog!

Eventually Jeanette cut the engine and pronounced the spot perfect.

We dropped our traps into fathoms and broke out the flask.

Guenda, guenda, guenda—the sound of a large diesel engine throbbed out of the mist, growing in intensity.

"Have we got any flares?"

"What for—we don't need help?"

"So we can alert the ship as to our presence," I suggested, figuring the flare might exit the cloud and be seen on the elevated bridge of a tanker.

"You're being silly, that's miles away," said my captain with conviction. "Don't worry."

Ten minutes later, the deep throb sounded deafening. I was convinced a giant bow was about to appear out of the mist; visibility wasn't more than forty-feet.

"*Kalimera*," shouted Jeanette, through cupped hands over my shoulder, nearly putting me in the drink. Her voice carried across the water.

"*Yassouooo*" came the reply; an alert crewman had heard Jeanette's call. The ship it seemed at least knew of another vessel in the vicinity. A large shadow chugged by moments later; an ocean-going fishing vessel. Afterward, it dawned on me that the fishing freighter would have had radar and been aware of our presence all along.

We exchanged a few shouted pleasantries and bearings.

When the mist finally lifted, we found ourselves well northeast of the island. Leaving our traps marked with a buoy, we headed for the nearest beach.

"The house is just up there, a three-minute shortcut," said Jeanette pointing up. "We can leave the boat here and go home for lunch."

Getting off the deserted sandy beach proved to be the first obstacle.

"The path used to start here," said my adventurous companion. "But it seems the rough winter seas have washed it away."

Indeed, exiting the shoreline appeared impossible as a small cliff, that ran the entire perimeter of the sand, hindered access into the jungle behind it. Erosion had chopped off any way of walking inland.

"Give me a hand with this driftwood—it might reach up to the top of the overhang." Jeanette had found a twenty-foot, washed-up plank. "I know where the path starts."

The makeshift bridge reached the root systems, which were protruding out of the eroded lip and we crawled up onto the "path".

We faced an impenetrable wall of bramble bush; the path was indistinguishable.

"It's also called *Fithi* Island in this region," she announced, as we struggled ear-deep through thorny foliage. "Snake Island, so it's advisable to make noise and carry a stick."

True to its nickname we encountered many on our slow advance through the dense brush. I was happy the place wasn't called Spider Island as eight-legged wildlife gave me the jitters. Rescue helicopters were miles away.

Three hours of bushwhacking later, up an incline, which often required the use of all four limbs, we emerged onto Jeanette's plateau scratched and weary. Even she admitted that going back down later to collect the boat seemed a little reckless. With it inaccessible and the pony in town at the bottom of the mountain, we had no choice but to opt for another march.

From the little harbour, we hitched a lift from a local fisherman to take us around the island to collect our dingy. Then we headed out to sea again in search of our buoy and hopefully dinner.

Three lobsters of acceptable length, half a dozen colourful but unpronounceable bony fish and an *octopothie* (octopus) went on the grill that night. A feast fit for exhausted expeditioners.

During the next two weeks I learned to wield a chain saw to some effect and even picked up a smattering of baking skills. There were no bakers on the island, so everyone made their own bread. I developed a taste for wild greens and weird fish.

"I think we will take the pony back to Ermioni," said Jeanette referring to the little town on the mainland opposite Hydra where we could leave the car. "Leon can have the back all to himself."

The little pony was labouring up the steep winding roads of Northern Greece, when we spotted a tortoise trying to cross the road. Suggesting that the little reptile might get run over, I insisted we stop and help it.

"The poor thing has already been run over," I exclaimed. The tortoise's shell was blemished, scratched and appeared slightly flattened.

"He seems fine though, perhaps we should take him back to Hydra and give him a good home."

I thought he would make an excellent companion for Felix. I'd nurtured Felix the tortoise back to health after being trodden on by Bluebell, my donkey of that period, which had reinforced my perception that a tortoise's armour can withstand heavy punishment.

So with the best of intension we put the flattened little tortoise in the back of the pony with Leon. That night we stayed in a small hotel outside Patras and I left some fruit and lettuce in the back of the car for my new acquisition.

I was a little disturbed to note in the morning, that my new pet hadn't touched the offerings and put it down to motion sickness.

"He'll be alright once he has a garden to play in," I enthused as we continued motoring down through the Peloponnese.

We stopped to stretch on a panoramic bend a few miles from our destination.

"I think I'll give Felix's mate a walk too," I said, lifting the little animal out of the back.

A recent thunderstorm had left a very large puddle on the side of the road and the reptile hotfooted it for the water, obviously thirsty.

When it reached the edge of the pond it carried straight on in and disappeared under the murky brown water.

"Do you think maybe your tortoise is a turtle?" asked Jeanette, laughing.

"It didn't appear to have webbed feet," I spluttered. "Poor little thing and now we have taken it hundreds of kilometres from his home."

I was concerned that it would be left high and dry once the puddle evaporated and I felt bad.

"Listen," consoled Jeanette, "remember we found him far from water and he seems to have a nose for it, so he'll be okay."

My reputation as a zoologist however was not.

Fossils and Foibles

A couple of the younger artists had found a bleached skull on the beach, two-feet long (including the beak) and about a foot wide. They had waded back to the ciaqui brandishing it with glee and puzzlement.

We had taken a group of Bostonian artists to the sandy beach on the mainland opposite Hydra in our usual ciaqui captained by old man Mikhaili. Everyone had been left to his or her own devises once we dropped anchor about fifty feet offshore.

Mikhaili was wizened and weathered brown with jet-black, dyed hair and a pencil moustache. It was rumoured that he was still skippering several decades past the legal retirement age. He was our favourite and his wide-beamed boat accommodated two-dozen picnickers in comfort. Her Barefootness, the dog-loving Countess, would generally command such outings and would adorn the picnic table onboard with exotic dishes. Mikhaili, suspicious of anything not rurally produced, was not to be seduced by "Guacamole" and the likes.

He had panache; with a white Panama hat pulled down over his nose, he would quietly siesta between sips of retsina and *tiropita* (cheese pie). He looked and played the part of the wise, experienced, old man of the sea.

He got up to inspect the find.

"It belong to a big bird from Afriki," he explained authoritively to the attentive group of students who had gathered.

I thought he was taking the piss.

I glanced at the students, a mixed bag of housewives, teenagers and graduates who to my surprise were nodding in awe.

Clearly this bunch were not remotely ornithologistic.

"A long flight for such a large bird," I chipped in, curious as to what Mikhaili really thought they'd found.

23

"Very old," he hedged his bets, waving a hand over his shoulder to emphasise generations. "Not now, before."

More nodding, he had just convinced a dozen East Coast urbanites, in fewer words, into thinking we now had in our possession a Peridactoral-O-Sourous find of magnitude.

I couldn't let him get away with it and morally it would have been wrong to allow these guys to go legging it back to their archaeological professors with such an "antiquity".

"What about the hole in its head?" I asked, offering him an out.

"It has been shot," said the pencil moustache, in a tone that implied any fool could see that.

Boston creative minds appeared to favour conspiracy and bobbed even more.

"Perhaps it swims?" I thought that would induce the Captain to re-evaluate his position.

"*Oxi, oxi*," wagged a brown finger, "palio, very old bird from Afriki."

"Okay then—what's the biggest bird in the world?" I could see that the authoritive tone of the Panama still held more audience appeal.

When a condor seemed to be winning in the ensuing debate, I suggested an ostrich, crooking my arm and making a loose fist.

"A skull about this size; seconded by an emu, which also doesn't fly."

An atmosphere of—"So?"—permeated the silence; Mikhaili peered at me over his shades unconvinced.

"All right then, if skulls contain brains, which is the most intelligent species of flighted bird?"

More debate, ending with my idea of a parrot perhaps.

"The biggest of which is a Macaw."

Again, the fist demonstrated a close approximate size.

"The biggest flying bird around here's a seagull, right Mikhaili?"

Mikhaili's lined forehead crinkled, eyebrows elevated skeptically.

"*Poli palio*", he insisted, we were back on the flying dinosaur kick.

When I turned the head over, dental apertures lined the "beak".

"Birds don't have teeth right?" I asked the inspectors.

I was really intrigued to see how far removed from the wild, these big city dwellers were.

"Dinosaurs had," said some diehards, still preferring Mikhaili's version, so I persevered.

"Fossils weigh a ton." I could see some nods had turned to frowns of doubt as I held the skull out.

"Feel the weight of this, hardly petrified."

"It's a dolphin skull chaps."

Silence, including the panama pencil.

"For this bird to fly it would need a wing span of ninety feet." More silence.

"The hole isn't a bullet wound but a breathing blow hole. And we know dolphins are extremely smart, hence the large cranium."

I could see the flying dinosaur theory was vanishing.

"Washed up on a sandy beach off a gulf that is known to have schools pass through."

I looked around for Mikhaili wishing to ask him when he thought firearms had come into use.

His horizontal, tilted panama was already snoring.

Sometimes I would take the helm for him and he patted me on the shoulder approvingly on the way back this time.

"We had fun today," he said in Greek, squinting at my course, oval cigarette clenched. "We nearly had them my friend."

Old man Mikhaili died of throat cancer a couple of years later and I never found out if I was the one ultimately "had". The "fossil" still adorns the entrance hall of her Barefootness' mansion, a fond reminder that leaves the question unanswered.

Was the old sea dog having me on, or did he himself learn a new trick?

Strikes and Stalemates

Before the Berlin wall came down huge chunks of EU financial support would flow into Greece and some of it trickled down as far as the Rock.

It was decided that Kamini merited a bigger harbour.

With the increase in yacht traffic, the main port was becoming too crowded in high season. It was reasoned that if another dock were constructed, some fishing ciaquis could then moor in the suburb, alleviating main harbour congestion.

The single Kamini pier offered no protected anchorage and had been used for summer inflatables and embarking only, nothing permanent bobbed.

A second convex wall about thirty meters out, sounded modest enough but at thirty meters the gulf dropped into dark fathoms. So a sea wall of some multi-story depth was required, a big job.

The proposal was approved and tenders applied.

It was decided to blow up Palametha for the raw material. For weeks massive boulders, hoisted by a floating crane, were dropped just off Kamini by the ton.

As with all grants the finances came with a deadline. A day when Brussels would want to see tangible evidence of their investment.

I would not be the first to observe, that Greeks have an ability of lulling one into believing they cannot meet a deadline and then, in a last minute blur of activity, they get the job done against all expectations. Generally it's all right on the night—

Eventually an EU suit announced he was arriving on Monday noon to inspect the new harbour. It was Friday.

The pile of jutting boulders didn't quite comply with the part that read "access road with bollards and navigation light".

A special license for a cement truck materialized with an unusual turn of bureaucratic speed. The whole island is a national monument and it is nigh on impossible to obtain a license for any form of vehicle normally.

I came back from Vlichos around 7.00pm on the Friday and builders were still hard at it, a big yellow mechanized barrel on their heels. The imported cement job was a fairly impressive machine it must be said. New, with tinted glass cabin set above the right front wheel and a small ladder to get up.

"They've got an inspector coming haven't they," Don said, leaning out of his window, which over looked the little port.

Nothing escaped his vantage and the construction of a new harbour on the island had historical implications.

Don is an extraordinary fellow, an Englishman, who hasn't budged from the Rock since he landed more than four-decades ago.

He is purported to have written six hundred and twenty-eight books, mostly by candlelight, because he refuses to see any advantage to electrifying his dwelling; a ram-shackle, little stone cottage with a concave roof and an outhouse with a selection of gypsy-like cages containing chickens and ducks, scattered in an adjacent, unkempt garden.

He likes the simple life and suffers from "remote-control-o-phobia", a sever handicap in this day and age. Push-button phones daunt him.

"I dunno," he would tut, his head shaking. "I like the ones that go round—a real dial—you know what I mean?"

This was his explanation as to why the phone didn't "work" while house sitting for a friend. He'd placed the handset upside-down and counter perpendicular to the rest.

But building stuff he knew about and was all too aware of the construction noise factor, which had suddenly disturbed his peaceful surroundings.

"All this time, good as gold they were," he tutted some more. "And this afternoon they didn't even stop for siesta."

On Monday morning, Don was up as I passed on the path to Vlichos, which climbs out of the little port.

"It's nearly done look, at it all weekend they were, amazing!"

The builders and their mates, with the aid of the four-wheeled monster, had slaved on the wharf non-stop.

Returning at lunchtime I could hear the rhubarb from halfway along the cliff road. A lot of people with opinion at the building site.

"Nearly drowned, didn't he," Don told me, leaning on elbows in the window. "Now how are they going to get that bloody thing up from in there—it was full you know—tons o' the stuff."

It took me a second to take it all in. A lot of gesticulated noise was going on around what appeared to be a bomb blast in the middle of the new structure.

"Someone thought a fishing boat may be underneath it," said the Bard behind me on the window ledge. "Maybe with a bloke in it."

A rectangle of four huge tires, about a meter below the surface, pointed skyward in the middle of the new port.

"The driver was trapped in its cabin, he only just managed to get out," Don went on. "Hadn't set had it—drove the thing on and half way down the wet cement sagged and collapsed. What a splash I can tell you."

The EU suit had arrived just in time to witness a semi-drowned driver being resuscitated and was met with an affidavit swearing that the structural slump would be repaired ASAP.

It was, as soon as the salvage operation was completed and the surviving cement and stones were dry.

Shortly after, an even bigger rhubarb developed surrounding the sudden appearance of another vehicle.

A bulldozer landed in Vlichos and started munching a road for itself along the cliff "road" to Kamini.

Civil wars have been started with less emotion.

As I've mentioned, all vehicles are banned on the Rock and permission for anything other than the two small garbage trucks is extremely rare; never mind one that was carving a path for more of its kind.

The demand for information grew loud.

Where had the beast obtained its papers?

Eventually an official statement was made, to the effect that "fire-breaks" were being cut, in the light of two big fires in '85 and '87.

Three locals had perished in the first attempting to rescue icons from a church on the hill when the flames had surrounded them. The second had almost incinerated a monastery. So the fire-hazard card had strong support.

The bulldozer was a fire preventive measure; the excavation in some parts of this firebreak was to allow access for a fire engine, it was explained.

A fire engine!

Conversation on the port rippled, tides formed.

"The thin end of the wedge I say, next it'll be a bus." A statement that guaranteed a hearty rhubarb.

"What fire engine—authorization for more vehicles is not written into the island's constitution."

"Anyway what good would one engine do even if it were allowed—ninety-nine percent of the Rock is in accessible—the only way to fight these fires is from the air—the way they've always done it," a pragmatist voiced.

"Prevention is better than cure—they should have a reservoir near the dump where the fires always start—more effective and cheaper than a road," came advice from the table behind.

"What harm would one little mini-bus do—it's their island—who are we to tell them what to do." The California end of the spectrum always cropped up.

"So the Brazilians can chop down the earth's last natural rain forest, asphyxiating all life, because it's theirs!" A tree hugger of different perspective gave our road an international status.

"One bus is hardly a rain-forest," defended the Valley.

Someone suggested laziness, another that a forest always starts with one tree.

"Don't they realize that this is the only thing left that makes this place special." More voice to stop the road rallied. "One little moped and this place is dead—it becomes like Poros, Spetses or any other island for that matter."

"Where else in the world, is there a town so close to a major capitol, which still runs on just donkeys," agreed another. "What would be the point of being here—It would become like all the rest, ruined by motors."

Debate flowed and ebbed, only decibels increased.

As the bulldozer progressed along the coast getting closer to making Vlichos accessible by car from Kamini, a lot of rhubarbs were fired off to the press.

Picketing the cliff road was mentioned.

"Human sit-down barricades"—even California had swapped sides.

The "thin end of the wedge" brigade, were threatening night raids with bags of sugar to stop the tracked monster. A kilo or two in the petrol tank was said to do the trick.

Eventually, the societies for the preservation of Hydra won and the Dozer was stopped—within sight of the new harbour.

But the rhubarbs over Kamini harbour however, didn't stop with its completion and indeed was the cause of further civil unrest.

The dynamiting for the new Kamini harbour wall had created a deeper access point at Palametha. Until then it had only been a semi accessible beach, for boat repairs, several furlongs further down the coast from Vlichos.

"An ideal place for building materials to be unloaded," said a gold shop owner.

The Merchant Lobby had long complained, that particularly in winter, the elegant, picturesque harbour front, looked more like a construction site and often hazardous to ambulant visiting tourists. A construction boat, the Agios Nikalous, would dump tons of building material on the port front. When it rained, mud would soil everything.

The Muleteer Union got wind of the proposition to use Palametha as an unloading point and lodged a complaint as well. Walking an extra third of the island to collect building materials would be too much of a burden on the beasts, not to mention the extra time and cost of delivery.

Some "preserve Hydra types" leaned with the Merchant Lobby and it was deemed that building activity must be conducted out of town.

The Muleteer Union took quick action. The following day, donkeys and mules stood in idle groups outside the municipal office and cathedral with placards attached to saddles in two languages, saying—

"Donkey on Strike! No fair, Palametha!"

Bemused oriental cameras clicked and locals postponed heavy shopping.

As the muleteers sat in a mid-port taverna supping beer and the island's sole transport system ground to a halt, the Merchant Lobby appeared to be stalemated.

But the Merchants' next move in countering the Muleteer Union's "victory" was to target the boat bringing in the building supplies. Its crane after all was responsible for dumping the piles of material—so no stuff on the port to collect, meant no donkeys on the port either.

That was the plan anyway.

Some paperwork arrived and a couple of uniforms were sent to enforce the banishment of the Agios Nikalous, cargo and crane vessel from entering the port of Hydra.

It was henceforth to be diverted to Palametha.

Gold shop doorways grinned as the small, still laden ship, chugged back out of the harbour.

The same merchants were amazed to see the scruffy cargo boat pull back into harbour in daylight the very next morning—bold as brass.

"Oxi! Oxi!" A walkie-talkie in a peaked cap wagged a finger at the mooring ship.

The moustache at the helm, stepped out of the bridge waved an official looking paper in one hand and continued to issue docking instructions with the other, ignoring the port authority.

Another couple of reinforcing uniforms were summoned; some gathered jewellery merchants egged them on.

The captain explained to the walkie-talkies on the quay that the boat was no longer his and that they should speak to his brother.

"*Vlepees,*" he said, pointing to the bow of the ship.

We looked. In rough letters, painted over the old embossed name, were the words—Agios Takis.

In order to prevent the boat from docking, a new court order would have to be implemented and legal proceedings initiated against the newly named ship, which now bore the name of the owner's brother.

Moons of red tape—stalemate again.

"Perhaps if we applied for another grant, then we could build another pier right in the middle of the harbour, exclusively for donkeys and Takis?" someone suggested.

It was a rhubarbless idea; it would solve the quandary and was accepted unanimously. The motion was submitted.

Money was raised and the extra quay finished without industrial mechanism, long before any suit was due to inspect.

And so it was proved that compromise could be reached and co-operation achieved, even here.

The Odds

One ripple of gas was all it took to start a cavalry charge and nearly wipe out half of the island's seven-year-olds.

I had offered to stand in and help Chris with the school's annual Christmas party.

"Simple," he drawled. Chris, from North Carolina, was an English teacher at the local language school.

"Their lesson can be writing letters in English and then we'll have a Christmas party for the class."

Music, refreshments, crisps, cheese pies, cake, sweets and balloons were assembled on the front desk.

The lesson part went well, apart from a small debate amongst the "teachers" about whether the "want lists" should be addressed to a North American "Santa" or an English "Father Christmas".

No sooner had the class been dismissed than a food fight started brewing at the tutor's table. I grabbed a packet of balloons and enticed the disturbance outside where it could do less damage.

The school was not too far up Donkey Shit Lane just before it got steeper. Flat enough for balls to materialize and games to grow, right at the express section for hoofed traffic.

A train came clip-clopping down the steps. It was unusually long, sixteen mules in single file returning from a building site on the hill. Four muleteers interspersed.

"*Yassou Vangelis,*" I greeted the first sidesaddle.

"*Yassou Pethia* (kids)," he beamed back at the children, completing the happy Christmas village scene.

I was standing in the school doorway surrounded by eager faces waiting for more balloons to be inflated and tied.

As the last mule plodded lazily in front of me, a large red balloon escaped as I was tying the knot. Pffrrrr—

This flying fart, spun insanely around for a while gaining velocity and then with its dying burst, went straight up the last mule's raised tail.

Big ears shot upwards and the surprised animal suddenly broke into a full gallop—straight into the mule in front of it, which in turn—

"*Malaka!*" yelled Vangelis, bouncing about as he struggled unsuccessfully to contain the stampede of his four into the squad ahead.

Like all good swear words, the inflection in how it is said, dictates the meaning and this time the M-word wasn't used endearingly.

Similar shouts echoed down Donkey Shit, as the entire train took flight, bobbing moustaches hanging on.

Island kids are as instinctive around donkeys, as city kids are with traffic; all had the good sense to stand against a wall.

Grateful that nobody got hurt in the stampede, I went to make peace with the drivers.

They were obviously under the impression that I could manifest such perfectly accurate flight from a flying balloon at will.

"*Oxi, oxi,* think of it like the lotto," I told them later in Dirty Corner, a favourite, local, hole-in-the-wall haunt at the bottom of Donkey Shit. "A million to one I couldn't do that again. And lucky too that no one got hurt."

Nods and orders, it was an against-the-odds luck of sorts.

Now would I help them with their lottery picks?

Things Just Happen

It sounded as though a donkey had just stampeded through the taverna kitchen. The crash of breaking glass and crockery drowned strumming bazookies. Then silence.

It was opening night at the beginning of the season in "The Garden", one of the island's biggest and most popular dining establishments—and it was packed. We had the added incentive to book a table because it was Lydia's first night and her boyfriend Jeff had promised we would be there for moral support.

"Lydia!" was the table's immediate response to the lull.

Lydia, a young, French, primary school teacher had hooked up with Jeff the previous summer and stayed. We had come to know her well over the winter.

Jeff was a fellow who had already extended his writing sabbatical four years beyond his original "six-month" schedule. An expat from San Francisco entrenched on the port and one of many "suspects" in the late 80's who resided on the Rock.

"That was what, three hours on the job," said Jeff, shaking his head. "Nearly a record!"

Lydia had tried her hand at a number of tasks. She was willing, bright and good-natured but was one of those few unfortunates whose life was a series of "things just happening to them". Accident-prone is a popular term for this syndrome.

If we were sitting inside, playing cards on a blustery winters day at the "Liako" and there was a domino-like shatter of falling beer bottles, then it was because Lydia's anorak toggle had snagged the one that was prime skittle. As ones *logarismo* (bill) was tallied at the end of the day by counting the number of empties amassed, these falling bottles could go on a while. Once, after an earth tremor, someone immediately suspected Lydia.

In short, the crash in the taverna wouldn't have gotten long odds on it being against the new employee's non-involvement.

Lydia emerged from the kitchen, looking forlorn, with her night's wages in hand.

"Ze tray jus sleeped."

"How many plates?"

"I don't know—forty to fifty maybe."

Jeff added a few to counter under exaggeration and still figured the restaurant was coming off worse financially our dinner included.

"You were lucky to get any wages," he admonished. "Now cheer up."

"Hey three hours isn't bad Lydia," quipped a second spoon, her attraction for minor disasters and short careers was semi-legendary.

"Eet wuzn't my fault," she stomped. "Eeet could 'appen to anyone."

We were all first hand witnesses to a few previous 'appenings and were somewhat sceptical.

It must be said that her accidents weren't all through clumsiness. Some people I have come to believe are especially selected to have machinery die on them; some devices may even hang-in-there just until a "Lydia" flicks the switch. Pipes about to burst waited until she was in the head, cassette tapes would be munched, etc. etc. But sometimes, she had a little hand in the bad luck herself.

Lydia was helping me to prepare a house for the General Manager of the Intercontinental and his wife, when this hand played a part. The couple were affluent part-timers, Germans, who drank designer water and had decided to make the island their weekend bolthole.

They donkied bottled water up to the house when most of us were content with the *glyco* (sweet) rainwater from the cisternas. Mrs. Intercon had an aversion to microbes and owned a pet Deutshund called Fritz.

"You clean up here and I'll take the downstairs and fire place." I knew not to leave Lydia in an area that might contain glowing embers.

"Just don't throw anything down the loo as it'll affect the eco-environment in the septic tank." Even those accustomed to using a bin for toilet paper sometimes forgot this aspect of island plumbing.

When I came up, the floors were wet and the smell of *chlorini* (bleach) could have put mortuaries to shame; it gleamed so we started putting the cleaning gear away.

"Where did you throw the dirty, chlorinated water?" I asked, noticing a general absence of puddles outside and dry flowerbeds.

"Down ze 'ole," she said, in an "obviously" tone and catching my glance she added, "I didn't want to kill ze flowers."

"What hole?" I smelled a rat.

"Zees one wiz ze lid, why?" She pointed at the fresh water, cisterna well-head.

"How many buckets?"

"Maybe five or six."

At an average of fifteen litres each, this meant at least a hundred litres of detergent into the drinking well—not well.

"Just as well they are micro phobic and drink bottled aqua," I said, hoping it would still be okay for showering.

Lydia and Jeff were my immediate neighbours.

Our apartments shared a kitchen wall and a large terrace. As I returned one afternoon, I noticed a small pall of smoke hanging over our house.

I found landlord Lefteris and a couple of neighbourhood moustaches standing hands on hips, surveying the smouldering remains of a double sprung mattress.

Apparently the *Koritisie's* (little girl's) bed had caught fire in the middle of siesta hour whilst she was still asleep on it. The source of combustion had yet to be established, but had the neighbours not been attracted by the billowing smoke and broken in to rescue the Koritisie, she might have been flambéed, not to mention the entire four-apartment block.

"She lucky, very okay, she go very quickly," they said.

The suspect had apparently made a marvellous recovery and escaped up the hill to a friend's house, not wishing to face Jeff without a satisfactory explanation as to why his newly imported, orthopaedic mattress was toast.

Jeff reckoned she was an insurance man's nightmare and he would regale us over breakfast.

"You guys won't believe what happened last night," Jeff would say, "she can't just have an ordinary flood like anyone else, no, she has to almost electrocute herself and blow up the building as well."

"Ze washer-macheen's door eez leaking," Jeff went on to mimic.

"Yeah and it happened to overflow down the hall across to the centre of the bedroom to where a hairdryer lay still plugged in!"

Some pyrotechnics and shrieking had ensued apparently as the house blacked out with a bang.

Like she said, it could 'appen to anyone.

During her stay she added colour to our society and she certainly did 'appen to us. A heart of gold and a way with kids—all of who fortunately had their own guardian angels.

Caviar and Moussaka

The donkey looked as though it had been shot gunned in the flank.

"*Po-po-poe, look my donkeys.*" The muleteer's right hand flicked up and down as he gazed upon his animals.

Indeed all six beasts looked like abattoir survivors. I knew from experience that this could be the opening for renegotiation in our transportation costs. The cleaning of half a dozen donkeys covered in red oil stain had not been factored into the deal.

"*Po-po-poe,*" I retaliated by gesticulating at the red splashes all over the carefully whitewashed entrance where eager hands had helped to carry the still dripping trays upstairs. My carefully manicured sweeping steps and arches, in preparation for what was supposed to be the island's party of the season, looked like carnage.

This gesture of solidarity put the moustache and myself in the same boat and we gave each other a *tea-nah-khan-amay* (whose silly idea was this anyway) shrug.

"Tasty stuff in red oil" is how a gourmet friend of mine describes Hellenic cuisine. Imagine dozens of traditional Greek dishes, metal oven pans loosely covered in foil, strapped on planks like stacked bricks, tied to the side of mules, wobbling up steep inclines aboard a wooden saddle—a recipe for disaster.

The damage looked collateral and guests were due to start arriving in ten minutes. It pushed stress levels.

I briefly considered fleeing and reflected on how I had come to be in this ghastly predicament.

"Joan would like to have traditional Greek food for her birthday party," the Sixth Beatle had announced a week earlier. Presumably Miss Collins was trying to be accommodating—when in Greece and all that.

"It's her fifty-fifth," he had added conspiratorially.

The guest list for her birthday bash was to include anybody who was somebody on the island's social roster. Joan accumulated a hundred new friends in no time and invitations had been sent.

Alexis Mardas would cordially like to invite you to Joan Collins' birthday party, RSVP The White Mansion. Phone, fax or send a runner, yours, etc.

Mr Mardas had approached me a couple of months earlier to say that Miss Collins was coming to stay in his mansion for a few weeks and would I be interested in a summer job.

Alexi had been befriended by John Lennon back in the days when the Fab Four were at the height of their fame and is referred to in Paul McCartney's biography as Magic Alex, on account of his skill with electronics. On occasion Alexi would bring out a pair of glasses, a guitar and other miscellaneous Beatle memorabilia.

"John wore these when we were in India together," he would say, always a crowd pleaser when table conversation dribbled. Hence, his acquired nickname amongst the expats of the Sixth Beatle.

So there I was on the splattered steps, moussaka and tzatziki for a ton of immanent, well-dressed guests, wondering whether we could still pull it off. There had been no way young William the resident chef, even with my able assistance, could have catered for so many in a house that sported forty-two phones (before the days of mobiles), a pool, jacuzzi, sauna, games room and five enormous bedrooms all en-suite; but only a shoe box for a kitchen.

The Sixth was a self-appointed tycoon, whose preference lay in obvious opulence. His house had been featured in numerous, illustrious "Garden and Home" type magazines but not in any "Kitchen's 'n' Cuisine" supplements, if you get my drift.

So the solution had been to cater out.

Invitations said 7.30, so if the animals were there by 7.15 we'd figured we could be squared away and serving cocktails 'n' caviar to the first arrivals in clockwork time. It was neither the done, nor practical thing, to have the food arrive during the event.

A various selection of a taverna traditionals, in vast quantities to go, on an island with no wheels represented a considerable logistical transport problem.

Tupperware was not an option as the dishes had to be served warm and carried in their heated oven pots.

Lamb, mince, chicken, keftethis, kalamari, beef, all generously basted in spiced red oil, covered only in foil and then tied on with rope. I doubted there could be much sauce left.

I surveyed the outdoor hallway in horror.

The Sixth would have apoplexy if he saw the chaos unfolding in the candle lit foyer; he being of nervous disposition and critical eye at the best of times.

Frantic activity ensued once the muleteer had departed, feverish, partially futile cleaning, the lighting made dimmer by extinguishing more than half of the candles and the strategic moving of pot plants over chronic smears, camouflaged the worst.

We were just putting the finishing touches to the buffet when the first group arrived. Still dripping from acceleration, we greeted the troupes with champagne in hand. None commented on the dimly lit foyer, nor reported slipping in any oily residue.

Apart from one almost catastrophic incident, the party went off without a hitch.

The Sixth, had insisted that three-foot, crystal, hourglass-shaped candle covers be placed at regular intervals along the hip-high walls of the main terrace.

A reveler, during a "rock 'n' roll" demonstration, bumped one of these heavy, glass ornaments off the wall. Naturally, it happened to be the one that was on the bridged arch above the mansion's entrance. A few seconds earlier and it could have decapitated a departing Dutch poet. For the rest, the night went well.

It was gone 3.00am by the time Willy and I had cleared up.

"Hey mate, I have a bottle of vodka on ice," said my exhausted colleague.

"What say we have a nightcap or two, I think we deserve to unwind."

In dribs and drabs family members and entourage would wander in for a morning bite. We had thought that on this particular morning we'd have time to recover with some strong filtered coffee first, as we suspected most guests would have a lie in.

Joan would normally be the first to rise in the morning. Fresh as a daisy, she would do her aerobics on the terrace and sup several cups of sweet, black coffee. Three or four teaspoons of sugar and lashings of caffeine might have had something to do with her vigour.

Willy and I were normally in better shape, but the morning after the party we were suffering from a lack of shall we say, energy. An empty bottle and sleep deprivation major contributing factors.

We were hopeful that Joan would sleep in for a change.

Oxi—fit as a fiddle, there stood Miss Collins before a drop had percolated.

"Morning boys, thank you for last night's party, you were wonderful and may I have my usual on the terrace please," she said with a dazzling smile, as she swirled out through the veranda doors, a stark contrast other household life.

A few minutes later, young William appeared on the panoramically bright terrace, carrying morning coffee.

He had severe DTs and the cup rattled alarmingly in its saucer.

Palsied and noisy enough for Joan to notice.

"Willy that's disgusting."

To which William replied without skipping a beat—

"Yes it is disgusting Miss Collins; you would think that Mr. Mardas with all his money, could afford crockery that didn't rattle."

Helicopters and Model Boats

"Goddamn chaos!" the bloke had drawled trying to push his way back out of the mass. He was holding what appeared to be a flying dolphin ticket.

"This thing will take nearly two hours," he was vocalizing to a waiting stretch limousine. "I can't handle that, I'm going to hire a helicopter to Hydra instead."

My ears pricked and I followed him back to the long car. Perhaps I could assist the bloke and convert my return ticket into his seat. I wasn't sure what I had in mind, only that he appeared to have a confirmed seat on the next flying dolphin (hydrofoil) and he wasn't going to use it. I hadn't a bean left in my pocket and didn't relish the thought of having to spend the night sitting on the dock waiting for the first boat back next morning, which was the earliest time my return ticket represented a confirmed seat.

I tapped on the tinted window and it slid down an inch. Suspicion emanated from within.

"I couldn't help overhearing that you planned to take a helicopter to Hydra." I was pleased to be dressed in travel attire and looked semi-respectable for a change. Island garb, T-shirt, shorts and beach sandals, didn't travel.

"Yeah?"

The Drawl was about to slide up.

He sounded Texan, presumably oil, judging by the size of the limo and youthful white Stetson.

"Who are you guys staying with?" figuring that I might know their hosts and have introductional credentials.

"Ain't stayin' with no one."

"I assume you have donkeys arranged—the helicopter lands at the cemetery on top of the hill—there are no cars?"

My tinted reflection remained motionless as this statement was digested.

"Yar joshing, right?"

"Absolutely not!" I said, in my best Queen's English.

"Y'all from around here?" Blonde hair loomed into the crack.

"Yes actually, I am a full-time resident of the island." I decided to lay it on a bit, "just flown in after a few days break in Venice, getting my return ticket endorsed now as a matter of fact."

Y'all loved the accent.

We got to talking after that. I explained that I had been self-appointedly marooned on the isle for some years.

It turned out that they had ultimately been heading for Myconos having just flown in from Dallas on honeymoon.

"So why Hydra?" I enquired.

"I remember someone saying it was also cool and was told to come here for a hi-drafoil."

"Not in mid-summer," I quipped. It was sweltering outside.

I joined them in the cool and discussed their options.

They had come straight through customs and had hoped to grab the next flight to Myconos.

"Is full," said the domestic flight desk, "all flights, until *avrio* (tomorrow)." But they weren't folk keen to wait around.

So they had decided on Hydra instead and had taken a long-cab to the hydrofoils, only to be confronted by a Greek rugby scrummage at the ticket office.

"One really should check the availability and book in advance for a helicopter, it will help with the hordes there as well," I suggested.

"I could make a quick call if you like, save you going all the way back to the airport and finding them fully booked too?"

"See Honey," Y'all enthused. "I told you we were lucky, this man is just what we need."

They gave me a name in case I was able to secure a helicopter; finances were not a major consideration.

He could have been related to a southern politician for all I knew, the vehicle certainly looked the diplomatic part and the hydrofoil office was most obliging.

"I need to order a *helicoptero* to Hydra for the American Ambassador," I fibbed, squeezing my way to the front of a mob, who were all determined to get back to the island that day.

Queuing is not a phenomenon known in Greek culture. In circumstances where there are only a dozen tickets left with a hundred punters bidding, matters tend to get loud. The only way to jump this lot was to pull rank albeit with someone else's fictitious credentials.

Pointing to the stretch limo with tinted windows behind the boisterous throng, I explained to the harassed cashier, that my client just had to get to the island that afternoon. So could she please phone Olympic Airways and see if a *helicoptero* was available, as this crowding didn't suit the *Keerios* (Mr) and he was seeking alternative transportation.

They obligingly booked a flight and I was told it would be ready to go by the time the *Keerios* got back to the *aerodomio*. I optimistically reckoned I had secured myself a seat on the last dolphin of the day.

I returned with the good news and enquired whether they would like me to call a donkey for them.

"It takes half an hour from the port for one to get up there." I had gathered these folk were accustomed first world clockwork. "Longer than the flight!"

I said I could arrange for one to be there when they landed.

I offered advice on accommodation; few hotels were air-conditioned then and gave them the general introduction rhubarb.

"Why don't y'all come with us, there is room on the helicopter right?"

An exhausted travel fund could leave one in an embarrassing situation, even if there was only minor funding involved, the inability to offer a reciprocal lunch for example but I saw my opportunity.

"No, no, you guys are on your honeymoon but I would be awfully grateful if you would give me your dolphin seat."

Perhaps I was going to sleep in my own bed after all.

"I could cash my ticket in and leave the amount at your hotel."

"Absolutely not," Y'all mimicked my accent. "Come as our guest, we're paying for the heli anyways."

"You saved our baycon, s'least we can do," the Drawl insisted.

In those days there were few phones on Hydra, so ordering a donkey was a palaver, one needed contacts. I called from the airport.

"Davey, I thought you were in Amsterdam, you aren't due back for another week." The Countess didn't siesta, so it was safe to phone her mid afternoon.

Everyone on the island knows each other's movements. It's part of the charm and at the same time, one of the drawbacks of living in a small community. One doesn't need to lock doors, but privacy isn't an option either.

"What happened, we were wondering whether you would survive a trip with those two?"

I told her Barefootness that it was a long story that I would explain when I landed, but could she grab a donkey and send it up to the cemetery for me in about three quarters an hour.

"You're coming by helicopter, I've got to hear this, consider it done. I'll send Miltiadis' mules up."

The helicopter's rotors drowned conversation.

As we flew in over the gulf towards the pictographic little harbour, toy town, I counted my blessings—home by a whisker and in style!

Another safari behind me and I thought back to how it began.

Tina had approached me the previous month and wanted to know if I would accompany her on a drive up to Northern Europe. Her vehicle's visa had expired and needed a trip abroad, to renew it or something.

"I know you don't drife in years, I just need a nafigator." Being half Israeli and part Dutch she had a distinctive, if unplaceable accent.

I accepted the offer to co-pilot a drive through Europe when she insisted a flight home for me was worth the security of travelling with a companion and was part of the deal.

"I am going anyway, so it will cost nothing—visit some friends along the way and we can fly back from Holland," she enthused. "Tree weeks maximum."

She possessed a pair of exotic little villas on Hydra overlooking the harbour entrance. Tina, regularly fluctuating in and out of the island community, was a noticeable presence on the port.

We decided to delay our departure so that Willy could work out his notice at the White Mansion and come with us. He had had a job offer in Amsterdam and saw this as his chance to escape the Rock for bigger pastures.

The Sixth had not been keen to see his prize young chef hotfoot it to the bright lights of Amsterdam. It ended with the young chef packing in a blur, garbage bags stuffed with pots and shampoo.

"We don't have to wait mate, Alexi said I could bugger off immediately." Willy turned up breathless at my place in the middle of the night. "Call Tina we can leave tomorrow."

William and I, not having the responsibility of steerage, celebrated our parole along the Corinth highway to Patras with a couple of refreshments.

The customs officials took a particular interest in Tina's car with its Dutch number plates and late dates. They then commandeered her passport; Willy's and mine were quickly checked and handed back.

A stream of large trucks flowed past into the massive hold of the ferry. If we were allowed on, it looked as though our fellow passengers would be mainly Italian and Greek truck drivers, with only a smattering of tourists.

"Look all these bic trucks going on," the pilot's patience levels were dropping.

"Doesn't matter, we'll be first off in Italy." I tried to inject a positive.

The uniforms had long poles with mirrors under the car and every stitch of luggage laid out in a row on the quay.

The hatchback was crammed with Willy's life and Tina's travel wardrobe. Several large designer suitcases and miscellaneous paraphernalia she wanted taken to her home in Holland all placed in single file next to the road, where the truckers drove slowly and inquisitively past.

Another uniform had gone in search of a sniffer dog.

Willy and I chatted and joked with them.

"Why you talking to the guards?" she growled at us, when they were out of earshot, clearly uptight at the delay.

"We only offered them a drink."

"What?"

"They're friendly blokes, it's Friday afternoon and this is their last shift."

"Are you crazy?" she hissed. "Now they will think we are trying to cover something."

Clearly our tactics differed.

When it was mentioned that our passports weren't the ones impounded, our shares plummeted even further.

Not a grand start. The dog eventually declared us free to embark shortly before sailing. Ours was one of the last vehicles to board the boat for the two-day voyage to Italy.

The ferry was a luxurious affair, complete with restaurants, shops, bars, a disco and a casino. We were sitting in the restaurant after dinner on the second evening, when I pulled three twenty-drachma coins out of my pocket.

"Might as well get rid of the change—I think I'll go and pop them in a fruit machine."

The slot machines were in the entrance room to the main casino, manned by a single cashier, in a cage.

The smallest acceptable coin to play was a fifty-drachma piece it seemed, so I went to the exchange box.

"Give me one fifty-drachma coin, *parakalo*," I said, placing my shrapnel down. "And keep the change."

"*Oxi*." The trimmed moustache behind bars wasn't very helpful.

"I just want to play once for luck, one coin, I don't even want a ten back."

"*Oxi*, only paper money." The fellow didn't bother glancing up.

"For fun, *parakalo poli*—"

An adamant, "*Oxi!*"

There wasn't a punter in the room so he didn't appear swamped.

I decided to see if I had any Greek money left in the wallet. All I had was a single fifty-drachma note.

No longer in mint, they were dwindling from circulation, but still tender.

"*Ena peninta coin parakalo*, with paper money," I asked, pocketing my three smaller coins.

He seemed hesitant to proceed with the transaction and I reminded him that he had stipulated paper money only. Clearly this wasn't the size note he had in mind. Not exactly a high rolling afternoon one could concede but still a punter with a coin, was better than no coin at all.

I walked over to the one-arm bandits and randomly selected a machine.

Aware of the watching pencil moustache, I inserted the coin.

One coin, one pull.

Bar—Bar—Bar

Jingling went on for a while, lights flashed, a passer-by or two stopped to investigate.

I took a coin from the pile and fed it back to machine, as one would tip a croupier and loaded my winnings.

Two pockets and a handful of change were dumped into the cashiers' stainless bowl.

"Be careful there might be three smaller twenties in there somewhere."

The moustache didn't twitch as some humourless rummaging through the change occurred.

Willy was most impressed when I returned with a re-padded wallet five minutes later.

William had originally come to the island as a teenager on holiday the same year I permanently moved to the island. I had just opened the bar and he had shown an interest in returning the following year to work. One gets used to hearing that a lot on holiday islands.

The following season young William turned up on my doorstep, with a girlfriend in tow, early one morning. I hadn't heard a thing from him since that mention the previous summer.

"My dear fellow all the prime positions have been nabbed over the winter by locals," I explained, as I brought them into the bar for tea.

Indeed I had acquired a staff of seven from half a dozen nationalities.

"Who cleans this mess up?" Willy asked indicating the bar, which was littered with bottles and dirty glasses. The floor still tacky from the previous night.

"I do." It was only a little bar.

"Well, we can do that."

And so William joined the islands expat community. He and his girlfriend understandably, didn't stick the floor-swabbing career for long and moved onto house sitting, before he slotted himself in as a house cook with the Sixth.

It had taken five years to extract him from the Rock, so our trip with Tina was a significant move for him.

As we sat down for breakfast on the last morning, the intercom announced in three languages that we were docking in Ancona; disembarking passengers were to have their papers and passports to hand.

Tina gave the disembarkation cards to Willy and told him to go hand them in while we went to the cabin to collect all our overnight bags. We would meet him in the departure zone.

There was no sign of Willy as we stood in the customs queue.

The customs disembarkation booth was busy trying to move human traffic and fingers clicked impatiently.

"*Disembarkation card parakalo.*"

"Did a young English boy give you our cards?" Tina asked.

"What?"

"English man, about twenty-three years old, brown hair, average build and height, was supposed to meet us here—"

"*Oxi, no card, no get off ship, we leave one hour.*" The uniform was impatiently emphatic. We lost our place in line and went in search; already the departure area was thinning.

"Go find him." Tina was beginning to get colour again.

There were few people about and I asked every employee I could find if they had seen my friend, as I searched up and down long, similarly lit gangways and decks. Soon I was asking for directions out of the maze having also lost myself.

By the time I got back to customs half the ship was on the lookout for Willy and Tina was again being detained. More colour glared, who could blame her, thus far help from the "nafigator and mate" had been found a tad wanting.

Eventually young William was seen sitting on an Italian bollard having a cigarette, looking lost. A sailor was dispatched to bring him back on board.

Willy had given the documents to the waiter at breakfast apparently.

"Why?" asked Tina's clenched teeth.

"I thought they were breakfast tokens—I even said to the bloke he could have them as we weren't going to use them—no wonder he gave me a strange look."

And when asked how he had managed to enter Italy without this card, "I showed my passport and—nothing, I just walked off," he shrugged.

More troops went in search of the waiter.

The steward never materialized. A further delay followed as new forms were found and filled out before we were allowed to go ashore. We were the last departing passengers to leave the ship.

"Willy, you carry the bags to the car meantime," said Tina, in a tone that left no doubt as to who was in charge of the expedition.

I waited until we got final clearance and then headed down the pedestrian ramp to join young William. Tina went down to the cargo deck to collect the hatchback.

"I think there's going to be a bit of a rhubarb mate," he said, looking sheepish.

"Why Willy?"

"You remember all those truck drivers who were chatting her up in the bar last night?"

Willy had appeared on cargo deck with the bags, to be greeted with much enthusiasm from exasperated drivers—fists, fingers and foul language out of windows. A small Honda was parked at the front of the unloading queue and was the cause of major traffic congestion.

Even for Tina this was going to be a tough one to weather. Truckers ran to strict time schedules.

Sure enough, we heard a gaggle of angry klaxons erupt from the bowels of the ferry; Tina had obviously just hit the cargo deck.

The little car came scooting off the ship chased by a convoy of huge honking lorries.

Her dark eyes were on stalks, knuckles white on the steering.

As predicted, we were indeed the first ones off!

Willy slithered silently into the unoccupied half of the back seat, I, the front.

Wheels spun and then the brake was suddenly stomped.

"What the fok is that." Clearly something else had touched a nerve.

She turned around and pointed to a large box blocking the back window.

"I got it in duty free," blurted Willy. "It's a radio controlled speed boat, Amsterdam has canals."

"Well I can't see out of the back window—there is no room—it will have to go." Whereupon she got out, opened the back and yanked the model boat off the parcel shelf.

She then marched over to a family sitting on their suitcases and handed Willy's boat to a little girl of no more than four.

"Prego, take, is for you, keep it," she said, then came steaming back, leaving a perplexed toddler clutching a big box.

"Be happy I still keep you in the car," she glowered at the rear view mirror.

Tina was silent all the way to Venice where she had decided we would stop for the night. But by the time we went out for pizza that evening conversation had began to flicker again.

Enter Carlos. A waiter of charm who took us under his wing.

Carlos was a keen fellow and most hospitable, showing us local haunts down back canals, away from the tourist traps.

In the days that followed, Willy and I were packed off to see glass blowing factories, museums, galleries—

Nearly two weeks later, Tina was talking about a real estate purchase in the city and had decided to halt any northerly advance, whilst negotiations were in progress.

Venice is a costly place and our funds dwindled rapidly.

Stranded, nearly penniless in one of Europe's most expensive cities, with no escape date on the immediate horizon, we opted to take matters in hand ourselves.

Willy had barely enough cash left for a third class train ticket to Amsterdam.

I packed him and a couple of armfuls of paraphernalia off; we wished mutual *kalo-taxithi's* (bon voyage) on Venice's station platform.

Then I explained to Tina that at this rate of travel we would be lucky to make Holland by Christmas. As my wallet was depleted save for a few drachmas for the taxi from airport to the Flying Dolphins when I got back, I was going to be more of a financial burden than help from there on.

Carlos, I was sure would agree that accommodation for three was excess.

It was decided to put me on the next plane back to Athens. I spent my last night in Saint Marco Square, ticket in hand waiting for the first water taxi to the airport and was saved a second night on the *dromo* (road) at the Athens end, by the fortuitous arrival of the long black car on the home stretch.

I left Tina, contemplating Venetian real estate, having learned the risks of leaving the Rock with a one-way ticket.

Four months later I bumped into her in the port on the day after she arrived back on the island.

The car was still parked in the outskirts of Venice, Carlos hadn't worked out and neither had suitable real estate been found.

"Do you want to come with me to pick the car up?" she asked. "That was quite an adventure we had—maybe we should do it again and go to visit Willy in his new job?"

"Via where this time, the Ukraine or maybe Poros would be the final destination?" I pulled her leg but I'm not sure she got the dry.

Royal Rhubarbs

"The King's Brother and Princess of Rhubarb are coming to stay at the Sixth's mansion and our chef has legged-it to Amsterdam," I implored Jesse. "And you're a great cook mate—"

I had been given carte blanche to find a cook for the royal visit.

As my culinary skills didn't extend past breakfast, never mind three weeks, we were in a bit of a stew due to Willy's escape. Skilled, unemployed gourmets were thin on the island at the height of season.

So I'd approached my old comrade, Jesse, a gent of girth and generosity in all matters. A fellow soul who liked variety in occupation—and he had flair in the kitchen.

"But the wife has her heart set on Rome-Paris-London and we're booked to go."

Jesse's extended vacation time had expired after eighteen months. The wife and baby daughter had reached their threshold of "life-on-the-rock" and were keen to see some other European sights, before heading back to Miami.

"Come on mate, the princess's sister is fantastic fun, I know her, plus you'll be reimbursed for the experience." I needed a mate I could trust for moral support as much as the production of menu.

"They are dinkum dynasty royals," I added. He knew I'd had fun catering a dinkum *Dynasty* soap-star earlier that summer. "How often in life do you get to meet blue bloods? The Eiffel Tower will still be there."

The deal was cemented when Jesse saw that although the White Mansion had a disproportionately small kitchen space, the Sixth had acquired every conceivable cooking gadget, some still unpacked.

"New toys!" he beamed.

The Sixth, as host, would get extra twitchy the day "special" guests arrived and would nervously fidget his way through the White Mansion alone, looking for lint.

Then we would walk through the premises together, him pointing out things for me to tell the maid, gardener or pool man.

Sparkling wasn't sufficient, one learned fine detail, sometimes buried in the closet.

I ran a finger over the top shelf and bottom corners, spotless, the princess's cupboard seemed perfect, I was curious as to what the flaw was.

To avoid future, tremendous embarrassment, clothes hangers were to be aligned. And the radio aerial compressed.

A gent with a discerning eye, so I had enough on my plate, without having to worry about what was going on other peoples and I was glad to have Jesse handling the Carte du Jour. He had scoured the island's markets, used every cooking toy and carefully prepared his introduction dinner. A meal fit for a King's Brother.

They'd a long day and were hungry.

Dinner was served on the white marble table outside under a lush, green overhead vine. Green-trim, designer cushions, green candles and white china.

I took the first course out. A chilled cucumber soup produced in a various selection of high-speed processors and garnished with a sprinkle of fresh basil.

Jesse was keen to know if anyone had commented on his first attempt as chef-de-royale.

"Excellent, delicious and can one of them have the recipe please," I assured him, the finest compliment one can pay a cook I thought.

He had worked hard to impress the regal appetites with the second course too.

Chicken breast, poached in a green grape sauce over rice, with a lightly sautéed zucchini dish and a fresh green salad. Artistically displayed on individual, hexagonal white plates.

"Oh man, there's no colour," exclaimed Jesse. "Everyone knows a plate should have balanced colour, at least a couple of carrots—too late now."

It had to be said, that the only thing thus far not green or white associated with the banquet, was the silver cutlery.

"Compliments to the chef again," I said to Jesse, as I went down to the storeroom to get desert.

Champagne and fresh honeydew melon sorbet in crystal goblets, garnished with a sprig of mint, made in the sorbet-making machine and served on a frozen white tray.

"They're going to think I am taking the piss."

"Stick a cherry on it," I suggested.

He looked at me incredulously.

"You mean as in, on-the-top—you're kidding right."

"Okay, if they mention anything, I could say you were colour blind."

He looked over his spectacles in disbelief.

"Or I could blame the Sixth—say that he told us green was their favourite colour."

I took the final course out not really as convinced as Jesse that anyone had noticed.

"In keeping with the colour theme throughout," said the Princess, as I placed the emerald desert in front of her. "How clever."

Jesse and I were to repeat our double act with the family in London and the Caribbean, when they ate more carrots.

Donkeys and Tortoises

The Sixth returned from the port one afternoon with his solution to my transport problem.

"*Ella Devid, I have brought you a present.*"

Alexi was standing outside the mansion's archway with a classic little brown and white donkey on the end of a rope.

"Somebody was selling her and I know you need help with the shopping."

Indeed, most would think the gift of a donkey on an island devoid of motorized transport, would be an asset. Something to be envied; especially when one was the major-domo for a tycoon with a flare for ordering in bulk.

"Where are we going to keep her?" inquired my horrified girlfriend, when I came home and tied the animal up to the front door of our little rented apartment.

Tortoises and snakes she had learned to cope with, but an animal of this magnitude, required serious housing. Ours was a small flat below the land folk, where we shared a small portion of their garden. A rabbit would have been crowding.

"What's her name?"

"That's up to us," I replied. "She's ours, a gift from Alexi, he didn't know her name."

"Lunatic," she snorted. I presumed she meant the Sixth.

"Where—how—who is going to house and feed her."

The girlfriend was an animal lover and had experience with large quadrupeds. She was more aware of the accommodation logistics than I.

"You shouldn't have accepted her."

But big brown eyes and pointed ears won the day.

She came with a saddle, a traditional wooden island type, complete with hooks for tying on paraphernalia and a corroded bell around her neck.

"Bluebell," chirped the girlfriend.

And so we negotiated a trial period with the landlord. Bluebell could inhabit the uncultivated area below our terrace—but we would have to find alternative accommodation in winter when she would need a roof.

That gave us about six months to find her a stable.

Unlike snakes and tortoises, donkeys need daily exercise, watering, feeding, brushing and some attention. A bored donkey can kick up an awful racket at any hour, including it appeared, favouring the much observed siesta *ohra* (hour).

The Muleteer Union quickly got wind of the fact that Bluebell had cut into their weekly pay cheque with the absence of grocery deliveries. The White Mansion at the top of the hill had been a regular fare.

I'd had Bluebell for about a week, when a large moustache purchased me an ale at the local, sat down and wanted to know my intent.

I knew it would be prudent to say that Bluebell was a pet, for personal use only.

No, I would not be meeting Mr. Mardas', or anyone else's guests off incoming ferries, I assured him. Neither Bluebell nor I, had any intentions of carrying luggage, in fact I would continue to steer arriving guests and any other transport jobs their way.

Another ale and a pat on the back secured the arrangement.

The Muleteer Union has strict code of conduct. They have taken one fellow to court for using his multi-lingual wife, to lure tourists into rides, claiming unfair advantage and breach of muleteering rules.

Bluebell proved to be more difficult to park than one would imagine.

Tying her up to the nearest lamp pole was quickly discouraged. Some trinket shop or taverna owner would get vocal as soon as Bluebell dumped on the cobblestones.

She also became adept at untying her knot and finding her own way to the local vegetable market.

Irate grocers on the phone became a regularity.

"You donkey eet all my fruits on display outside, come, get it now." Most embarrassing.

Donkeys are not allowed on the port after dark unless for the express purpose of meeting a suitcase off a boat. So night "walks" were off the menu too.

The White Mansion was too well groomed and had no appropriate place to keep the animal during work hours, so she was returned to the garden after each shopping trip.

Bluebell decided that the carrying of humans wasn't something she intended to do either. One is supposed to sit side saddled and indicate direction by gently pulling the chin rope. Except in Bluebell's case one could yank her head backwards and she would still brush the leg side against a wall.

So Bluebell spent most of her time, happily prancing around the enclosed patch of land, which she shared with Felix the tortoise and at least one grass snake.

These reptiles had found their way home with me during walks in the hills. Felix loved scraps of apple and lettuce and would wander up to the front door a couple of times a week for a snack. An endearing little fellow, about the size of an oval grapefruit; he walked, fed and amused himself.

I noticed that Felix hadn't appeared for his treat one day and searched the garden. I found the poor animal, his geometric shell cracked and crawling with white maggots. A chip, the size of a donkey hoof, had caved the centre of the tortoise's shell inwards. He was alive as I carried him up to the girl-friend—but only just.

Felix made an amazing recovery.

After we had picked the visible parasites out with tweezers the chemist had advised us to swab the cracked shell out with bicarbonate soda. Felix would prop himself against the wall to catch the maximum, recouping spring sun; we made sure he had plenty mashed fruit and was henceforth barricaded into the safety of our little patch.

I reported the Bluebell accommodation problems to the Sixth; a wonderful pet and we loved her dearly, but not a practical tenant in our circumstances—thanks all the same.

"Take her to the stables in Molos, she will be happy there," he suggested.

Indeed Molos had space, acres of it and proper stables. The only trouble was that Molos was usually only accessible by sea, a secluded bay, halfway along the west side of the island.

The little donkey was ceremoniously saddled up for the long hike. Walkman strapped to the front of the saddle, an ice chest and picnic gear tied to the pommel. Jesse and I took the day and Bluebell off. Getting her down the goat paths to Molos bay was not quite as precarious as I had anticipated and we left her happy in a retirement paddock.

The next time I saw the large moustache I reciprocated a pint.

"*Po-po-poe*," I exclaimed, sitting down next to him.

"*Mularia poli thoulia* (work)," I said, explaining that after so much *fassaria* (trouble), Bluebell had been sent to live in the country.

"*Bravo sou*" he said, grinning. I was lucky to be rid of her, too much fuss he agreed.

Twelve years later, I had moved back into the same neighbourhood, a house below the same patch of unused land where we had kept the menagerie, except that by then, it had been cultivated.

I bumped into Ed at the Four Corners supermarket one afternoon, Rebettica Ed, a gent who I knew from my days with an e-mail shop on the port.

He was still in need of cyber assistance so I invited him home with me so he could check his e-mail.

I was leading him back to the house when I saw, walking directly towards us in the middle of the lane, a tortoise about the size of a rugby ball.

His shell was missing a chunk the shape of a half moon.

Ed had followed me onto the terrace somewhat bemused by my enthusiasm over a tortoise.

"Sorry Ed, Felix and I go back a long way, I probably saved this guy's life back in the '80s and I haven't seen him since."

"Girls come and meet Felix," I bubbled, as soon as I got in the door.

"Hello Felix, nice to meet you," said Kelsey my wife, as she walked out with courteous hand extended and greeted Ed.

"No, not him—here Felix—still alive after all these years," indicating the large healthy tortoise walking across our terrace.

Mices and Men

The island has a knack of doing the unexpected; sometimes sabotaging the best laid plans of mice and men.

Having turned my hand to a number of tasks, I had thought that accepting the offer of longer-term employment in a secure environment was a step forward.

I have mentioned a couple of the memorable events from my involvement with the White Mansion but the first rhubarb happened only an hour after I arrived for work on my first day.

The interphone went. I had assumed it would be the Sixth requesting morning coffee and a welcome chat.

"Devid, I have just been woken by the Chief of Police who wants to see you in his office now—with your passport," said my new boss, sounding understandably irked.

"Why Alexi?" I asked, genuinely perplexed. This was the first such summons I'd ever had and the inclusion of "passport" had a bad ring.

"He didn't say—he was pretty upset—you had better go down now."

Impressive start, I thought. I couldn't figure out what had induced the Chief to trace me to the mansion only minutes after I had turned up for the job.

I racked my brains walking down the hill.

The only possible rhubarb I could think of, which would involve the law, was over a small rental disagreement. Just a favour I had done for an acquaintance a couple of weeks earlier. The passing on of a useful phone number was all.

A subsequent encounter with a mouse and said tenant had caused some grief but I didn't imagine for one minute, that this merited sufficient importance for Police Chiefs to be calling Tycoon's before breakfast.

I tried to recall the events surrounding this issue just in case that was what the summons was about as I searched for the passport.

The securing of discount digs for three months during the height of season is no mean feat. A studio with a view, kitchenette, private bathroom and private terrace for sunbathing. I had thought she'd love it.

She didn't and had moved out after a couple of days. There was an ongoing rhubarb over the deposit and the manager was away.

Blondie did have a point; there was no small print in the rental contract that covered wildlife invasions.

No clause in the agreement that mentioned full re-imbursement in the event of a mouse and a miceophobic tenant meeting under the sink, which had resulted in fleeing and damage to property, mental, and physical health.

She had been most insistent that she couldn't wait until Jeanette, who managed the house, to return and was adamant about instant reimbursement.

So I had approached her Barefootness with the problem as she was a co-agent and also a friend of Charles the LA based house owner. Plus Jeanette and the Countess were close buddies.

She had agreed to pay Blondie and Jeanette or Charles could repay her later.

"Tell her Monday morning, outside the bank," her Barefootness had said. I did and had thought matters were placated.

On the Sunday evening, relaxing on our terrace after a boat picnic, her Barefootness wanted to know the inside story.

I explained about a mouse being the cause of all this fassaria.

"A mouse—the cheek, she's a big girl—what about the lost bookings from people we turned away—well I'm not paying her."

The rhubarb had really started to get into full swing when I had been sitting at the "Three Brothers" and Blondie had come thundering up to my table, the second day after she'd moved into the apartment.

"Mices in the room," she panted, "I didn't sleep and had to go to the doctor, I have blood pressure and had heart palpitations."

Little field mice were fairly common on that side of the hill, so I wasn't all that surprised.

I'd thought she might have been kidding; anyone half as familiar with the Rock knew that rats and roaches exist.

"Mouse singular—mice many honey—how many?" I tried to lighten the crisis.

"At least one."

I'd laughed. "Don't you get mice in Tel-Aviv?" And got a scowl in response; my humour had failed dismally.

I'd made amends, marching up the hill with her, to purchased poison pellets from Four Corners. I'd sprinkled a few under the sink and explained that this made them go to sleep, somewhere outside where they dehydrated, so stuff didn't rot and things.

I'd left, feeling sure that the matter had been appeased.

I'd seen her a couple of days later.

"All okay?" I smiled.

"I moved out, I found ze dead mices, so I go juz like that," she said, distraught.

The mouse had chosen not to die out under a bush but elected instead to perish in the centre of an ornate salad bowl.

She had opened the cupboard sink the following morning and found the ex-mouse.

"I couldn't touch it, so I throw ze bowl out ze window."

Three stories up, lucky I thought that there were no pedestrians below.

The fact that large, stone, semi-resided houses on Greek islands sometimes attract little mice was not a good enough excuse.

"I come for 'oliday not to 'ave zees stresses, I want my deposit back," she had demanded. Enter my call for backup.

The following morning, I called her Barefootness to check there hadn't been a change of heart.

"I haven't changed my mind she can go and jump, Jeanette will back me up too."

Blondie had waited for a futile hour outside the bank apparently and then went straight around to the precinct.

The chief uniform on duty had been obliged to phone the Countess there and then.

"Absolutely not Gregori, she cannot demand like this, she must wait and talk to Jeanette. Or she can phone the owner in LA, if she wants." Click.

The cop told Blondie so she had stormed out in search of me.

Later that day, Felix bellowed to me from his usual elevated table at the "Three Brothers".

Felix was a Norwegian novelist, not to be confused with my tortoise. He had semi-retired to the port front cafés of Hydra and had become the replacement rent for the plaintiff's vacated studio. Felix was a rare commodity, and his presence brought a lot of flavour to the island, a jovial fellow, with wispy hair and no aversion to mice.

Felix possessed a unique intellect, with humour and a distinctive style. He would attract an audience wherever he sat. Impeccably spoken, in a gold waistcoat, waving a long cigarette holder he would blurt out whatever came to mind, sometimes preceded by a distinctive windup chuckle.

"Halloo David, yuk—yuk—yuk, the blonde battleship is looking for you," he called, referring no doubt to the plaintiff's considerable bulk.

I thanked him for the warning and headed up.

I had already told Blondie a dozen times, that Jeanette would deal with it when she returned from Othonis. As the funds were banked, I had no say, or access to the account, so couldn't do any more. This was a favour rapidly going wrong. It's unpleasant having to avoid one's usual haunts because of rhubarb on the loose.

"Battleship?" It hadn't taken long for Blondie to get wind of Felix's quip. "What is zees?"

"Large," said a spoon, at her breakfast table next morning.

"Megalo," confirmed a second, stirring.

Digestion took a couple of seconds.

"I know anuzzer battleship, I'll give zem battleship," she'd fumed, steaming off to the coppers.

With mutters of embassy involvement, she'd staged a sit down protest in the chief's office. Threatening not to budge until she had her money.

"Wezzer from Zanette, David, the Countess or Felix," she didn't care. She had a flask and lunch on hand.

Such bulky anchorage, discouraged any thoughts of physical eviction. So the early morning phone calls were made.

Some people are not known for their demure negotiating skills and Blondie was no exception.

Not only did she perceive herself to be short-changed but apparently she also felt she had now been *twice* insulted.

My guess was right; the mices had conspired, culminating with the call to the Sixth. By the time I had collected my passport and arrived at the station, I found her Barefootness, Felix and the Battleship all talking at once and the Chief staring at the ceiling.

Actually Felix was chortling loudly, slapping his thigh and saying things like "isn't this wonderful." Felix loved theatre and he had the best seat in the house.

The bespectacled, stand-in police chief held our passports up, clearly frustrated with his inability to take control of proceedings unfolding in his office and he had to raise his voice above the noise.

"Okay, no passports back, nobody!" This got instant silence. "Until everybody shake hands and be friends." More silence.

"*In front of me*," a pause and he emphasized, "*here, now, or I keep passports.*" The paperwork would be enormous if nobody shook.

On the one hand there was the Barefoot Countess, whose connections were at the top of any ladder and on the other the Blonde plaintiff, her embassy and the formidable Tina as her ally if need be.

"Jeanette is in charge of the house, she is in Othonis and is coming next week so it can be sorted out then," said her Barefootness, presenting unity with the Jeanette and her considerable local influence. Island solidarity and the longevity of landownership point, being made.

"No, I stay here and until I get my money you can keep my passport," declared the Battleship, determined to remain at anchor.

Her Barefootness started to site the names of powerful lawyers.

"Yuk, Yuk," the Chortle chipped, "all this for less than two hundred dollars; isn't it marvellous—one couldn't write such a script—yuk, yuk."

Gregori and a couple of his uniforms looked helpless in the face of this standoff.

He took off his cap and looked imploringly at her Barefootness.

"Parakalo Madam, pay her, for me, I would myself but it is not allowed—"

Eventually hands were shook and passports returned once finances were settled.

I headed straight back to the White Mansion.

"Hi Alexi, you'll believe what that was all about," I said. The Sixth was sitting by the pool when I got back.

"I know Devid," he said looking sagely over shades. "This blonde is tough, she beat you all, using one little mouse."

Monastery Monster

"Hey man, check this stone carving out. It must be centuries old!"

Our excavations had already unearthed two layers of floor. Under wooden planking, we had discovered ceramic tiling and now it seemed there was a third possibly original floor made of sandstone slabs. The piece that Lourens had exposed was hand carved presumably by ancient monks. A cross with old Cyrillic script.

Lourens and I were working at the top of the hill on the restoration of an old monastery above the harbour. Even at that elevation one could hear recognisable noises echoing up from the port. The amphitheatre's effectiveness does wonders with the acoustics; one can hear phones ring in the evening quiet.

Lourens, a gifted artist from South Africa, looked and behaved like a combat veteran of that continent's old bush wars. The kind of fellow you want on your side if you were going to be mugged or doing heavy manual.

One aspect about living full time on the Rock is that the cast changes continually and as a result long-term inmates tend to withhold themselves from the holidaymaking throngs and be more selective about those that stayed.

The syndrome is well-known—close vacation friendships and promises to write, become ever more infrequent postcards—a bit pointless if one is living in the postcard.

A colonial voice on the port once said "I never speak to anyone unless they've been here for at least two years."

At the time I thought it snobbery but over the years have come to understand what she meant.

If a new personage was still around after the awnings and chairs were gone, then the chances of making their better acquaintance rose considerably. One got to know people over a winter, bonds developed.

Sadly most mates don't do more than a couple of years on the island before the lure of the First World entices them away again. So one becomes hesitant about building bridges.

"There's a South African painter who is thinking of staying here the winter, perhaps you should meet him?" said a Canadian pipe, at the table next to me. He knew I had some history with that part of the world.

"Well, let's see if he does first, shall we?" I was even more disinclined than usual. The last thing I wanted was to find myself discussing that country's political dilemma. I had given up on its policies in frustration, along with the rat race, years before.

"That African bloke is still here, he seems quite nice and he's heard about you," said the pipe, some time after the first rains.

"What sort of South African, they come in many shapes and sizes?"

"White, looks like a mercenary" he had puffed.

This sounded ominous, "Language?"

"Strong accent, Afrikaaner I think." The pipe obviously didn't know what a Boer mercenary type potentially represented. Mr. Mandela was still in jail. Something akin to being asked to befriend a Nazi in 1946.

The following day, an unkempt muscle with stubble sat at the taverna table next to me sketching on the paper tablecloth. A few pints later we discovered we were in the same political camp and so I befriended a human bulldozer.

Lourens became my working partner. No "handy man" job to large, including the dismantling of old monasteries.

He would add pencil sketches to our documentation of the dig if we unearthed anything of interest during the day. The carved flagstone merited a drawing so we downed tools, as it was late afternoon anyway.

Just as we were sitting down to enjoy an after work cigarette, before clambering down the mountain, we heard voices somewhere in the valley below us. They carried clearly in an unfamiliar, singsong language. It was rare for anyone to come *up* the deserted hill at dusk, even for locals.

A large, arched doorway dominated the entrance of the ageing structure. Heavy wooden doors, held together by a thick rusted padlock and chain, gave it a desolate look. A great location for a scary movie!

Lourens and I peered through the crack between lopsided doors and were amazed to see three Japanese tourists out exploring. Over nighters' from the Orient were rare as it was seldom that any of their groups stayed for more than the allotted hour off the cruise boat.

A guy with a camera bag and two elegantly dressed ladies were ambling gently up a disused donkey path towards us. Lourens put a finger to his lips as we watched their progress.

When they were about thirty meters from the entrance there was a sudden guttural roar over my shoulder. Simultaneously, Lourens had grabbed the doors and begun shaking them violently. The chain rattled dramatically. Puffs of masonry fell.

I nearly had a heart attack and I looked down at the hikers.

They'd stopped dead in their tracks; the woman hands to their mouths apparently stifling, the fellow dropped into a crouch staring at the monastery, jaw on the path.

Lourens let rip with a louder second rattle and roar even more fearsome than the first. The visitors fled and I feared for their ankles as they bounded back down the precarious slope.

"That was really mean," I told him.

"No man, just think of the story they can tell their mates back home, they'll always remember this walk," he said grinning. "Now they've had a real adventure."

"You do realise that not all tourists feel that encountering a Yeti in a haunted house is an essential ingredient to their "adventure holiday" mate."

"Ja, but now they have something to tell their kids. I bet you they always recall Hydra before the Acropolis even." Lourens had a habit of looking at things from a different perspective.

Lourens' daughter started going to the local kindergarten and one lunchtime we were sitting at the "Three Brothers" watching her and a gang of kids squabbling over some pencils on the steps outside the taverna.

"Listen to my little girl man, she's really picked up the language in just a few short weeks," he said, beaming with pride.

"Do you know what she is saying, old bean?"

I explained that her language translated would have made *him* blush. He shouted at her in Afrikaans to stop.

"*Lollie, moonie, moonie, kom heer,*" which caused a stunned silence amongst the Greek diners.

Lourens sensed the disapproval from adjacent tables.

"What's the matter with them, hey?" he asked.

"You have just called your daughter with the Greek word used for the crudest description given to a female sexual organ. They probably reckon you're trying to top your daughter as a linguist," I laughed.

Lourens begged me explain the faux pas to the frowning moustaches.

"Strange language Afrikaans," said one.

"No wonder they say it's all Greek to me," answered Lourens.

Last known, Lourens had married an English wife, survived a serious bout of throat cancer and held several successful one-man exhibitions of his work in a number of countries.

Sewage and Cement

Georgo needed a hand to clean up the street outside his house.

"There are some cement splashes that need chipping off and my back cannot cope," he explained. "Just a little job."

Georgo owned one of the island's grand mansions, situated high above the port, in the labyrinth of the upper town's cobblestone streets.

According to Georgo, he had solved his on-going problem with a leaky *vothros* (septic tank) in the neighbourhood, by blocking the hole with cement. For some time there had been a rhubarb about a stagnant odour that wafted through the area. Numerous complaints to the Municipality and police on the issue had been made by a various selection of plaintiffs.

Georgo had return from the Big Olive that spring and decided to fix the problem for once and for all.

"How much cement did you use?" I enquired.

"Fifteen bags," he said, with the surety of a man who knows that fifteen bags of cement would block a flood, never mind stop a leak.

I swept the street before attacking the few cement spots with a hammer.

"*Tee kanees etho?*" I was used to black-shawled yayas (grandmothers) coming to investigate whatever proceedings were going on and asking what one was doing.

But this yaya didn't seem pleased with my answer of helping Keerios Georgo tidy the road and started to babble and gesticulate.

"*Oxi, oxi.*" A waging finger indicated that I should cease work. I was accustomed to free advice and experience had taught me not to pay too much heed. I suggested to the old dear that she take the matter up with the house owner and continued chipping.

She banged on the massive front door. I assumed that Georgo was deep within the rambling house and hadn't heard the knock when she got no reply. She waddled off, muttering.

A couple of minutes later she returned with reinforcements. Three yayas, all shouting at once! My efforts to improve the street were not getting the appreciation I had hoped. I reiterated that Georgo was the man they should be talking to and continued filling a rubbish bag.

Yayas may appear like helpless little old ladies dressed in black just being nosey but are in fact, the real authority in island society. Yayas know who, where, why and what about anything that moves in the neighbourhood. They have an information network bar none and troops of family to enlist if required. One does not argue with yayas.

The noise attracted more people none of whom seemed pleased with what I was doing. I started to wonder that perhaps I was encroaching on Municipal territory and therefore not entitled to work on public domain. I told the growing mob that I was merely the assistant; complaints should be directed to the employer. More rapping on the door failed to get Georgo to materialize.

I caught the word *astinomia* (police) during the debate. Someone else mentioned the *Demachio* (the Mayor). Still I wasn't concerned. The Mayor knew me. He spoke English and most importantly knew the influential estate owner for whom I was working.

I had almost finished when two uniforms arrived and declared my labours illegal. I was officially requested to relinquish the hammer.

The whole neighbourhood had assembled by this stage and I suppose I shouldn't have been surprised when the balding dome of his Mayorship puffed into view. Good I thought, he could translate and explain to the irate locals and police, that I was merely an innocent labourer.

"*Tee kanees etho?*" asked the glistening dome, pointing to my bag of rubble, his air of authority silencing the rhubarb.

"Ah, Mr. Mayor glad you're here, just helping Georgo tidy the street," I said, hoping that he would view my task in a favourable light.

Where upon he burst into emphatic Greek from which I was able to glean, that he too, had sided with the mob and had suddenly lost his linguistic skills. By now I was perplexed. Where was Georgo and why was there a lynch mob gathering over a bit of sweeping?

My Greek isn't that good but it was abundantly clear that the demand for me to report at the police station, with passport, was included in the rhetoric.

"Mr. Mayor, I know you speak English, what's all the fuss, am I not helping the municipality do its' job?" I retaliated.

A statement which failed to provoke a conversation in my mother tongue, but instead produced a stream of Greek, which sounded very much to me like *tampering with evidence*.

A couple of black shawls were trying to lead the Mayor further up hill. The fifteen bags of cement had created a dyke, it seemed, which was backing the sewage up.

Behind Georgo's mansion, houses were apparently awash, someone had fallen ill and it was thought that plague was immanent.

Unblocking the drainage would take dynamite one pointed out. Others suggested using the explosives in a less productive manner. The Mayor gave me another verbal reprimanding, in Greek, for the benefit of the crowd.

I'd had enough.

I downed tools and hammered on the door. Surely Georgo must have heard the noise in the street by then.

He eventually appeared and cast assurances to the throng that the problem would be taken care of officially. My endeavours were merely temporary cosmetics to win favour with the local populous, whilst the real matter was being investigated.

Some further dialog ensued, the upshot of which was that his Mayorship did not grant me further leave of labour and with what I took to be grunt of dismissal, I dispersed with the rest.

Later that afternoon, I bumped into the Mayor on the port.

"Hello David, how are you, nice day we're having," he chirped, his English remembered and the morning's event forgotten.

The Breakfast Club

"You no more order omelette here!"

My friend Eva, the owner of one of my favourite tavernas, was apparently banishing me from the "Breakfast Club".

I had been an executive member, achieved for excellence in paid up attendance—about six breakfasts a week for half a decade—winter and summer.

"Your omelette just cost me several thousand Drachmas," Eva said, laughing but clearly there was a matter of profit loss to be discussed here.

Later, the ever-cheerful Eva added in her amused manner, "we must talk."

Beneath the banter there was an obvious need to renegotiate my membership rules.

As far as I knew, I'd never run a tab with her for more than 24 hours.

"The Liako", was my combined breakfast club and office. It would be akin to banishment from the menu at one's clubhouse.

Eva knew how hard it was to eke out work at times and that half my average daily budget, about five-hundred-drachmas, would be allocated to occupying a seat at one of her tables, sometimes—most times—for hours a day. At forty-drachmas a pint and the same for eggs, one could park for considerable time on a fiver.

I went principally for the port-front theatre; eggs and beer were the entrance fee. The island breakfast club, open morning till late at night, three hundred and fifty-five days a year.

The hub for expats, part-time or year-rounders, tourists and locals alike.

A polygamy of nationalities and backgrounds.

Eva would serve anything, under or over the grill, at all times, in the days when nobody raised an eyebrow if beer was the "beverage de preference" before noon.

It was my lounge and it had a phone. A lot of us waited years for a line.

71

During the previous, tough winter, Eva had been an immeasurable ally, in my rivalry with the port front cats.

When a gent is earning five-hundred "drachulas" an hour for sporadic menial labour and watches the port cats snag a weeks worth of earnings off adjacent tables as soon as the Japanese tourists stood up each day; he gets to thinking.

Who was supposed to be top of this food chain?

Perfectly good, tasty, untouched *kalamari* (squid) and prawns, at a value well above the daily winter budget, being devoured by the same toms who regularly sprayed one's shopping or coat tails.

This was territorial stuff.

"*Kah neechie-wah,*" gold shop owners would greet the island's only winter tourists, ninety-five percent of which hailed from the Japans.

The Hermes "three-islands-in-one-day" cruise boat affectionately nicknamed the Herpes as it would blight our view of the opposite side of the harbour, would disgorge a couple of hundred, for an hour each afternoon.

The Liako was the first taverna the tourists walked into as they got off the boat and obviously the last before they re-embarked.

Many would be attracted by the dead *octopothis* (octopus) Eva would string up alongside the tables and they would sit down ordering her finest seafood.

At least one table would hustle off leaving substantial parts of their lunch untouched.

No sooner had they got up than three-dimensional fur and claws would swoop and skedaddle with freshly grilled tentacles. One needed tactics.

A quick glass of thrown water usually kept the competition at bay until it was socially acceptable, that is the gangplank had been traversed, to lean across to the next table for first dibs on the morsels.

Eva had apparently been privately watching my maneuvers with some amusement.

"*Oxi, wait,*" she tutted one afternoon as I had sidled over to the barely touched plates. "*I take.*"

Five minutes later, she'd come back out with a seafood platter. My "leftovers" on a fresh plate and re-heated. A feast fit for an executive of the club.

Prawns on rice, fresh octopus on the side—the day's rescuings.

I dined well that winter.

But now it was going summer—the rules had changed is seemed.

I decided to square this away with Eva. One shouldn't cost the innkeeper money to be frequenting their establishment, especially when they have been so generous.

"Ella Eva, what?"

It transpired that the boys had been splashing out on breakfast, until my arrival.

The club's "A-team" breakfast table that day had a hankering for lobster, prawns, some salads and mezes. All was written down—

"I'll just have my usual please Eva," I had chirped at the end of the extensive order.

"What's your order?" the banker inquired.

"Eggs."

"Actually, an omelette does sound much better, a heavy lunch in the sun isn't a good idea. I'll just have what David's having as well Eva, *parakalo*."

Me too—had echoed around the table—

From then on, I simply got a "cat-plate" if I was in the company of well-heeled appetites and always left *avga* (eggs) off the menu, winter or summer.

The Liako stayed open for over a decade. Eventually human traffic from offloading tour boats pressurized the ambiance; the advent of phones in every home and most influentially, the introduction of a few dozen television stations changed the way we lived and dined on the Rock forever.

Subs and Slugs

"It's like James Bond," said Günter, peering at footage that the miniature submarine was beaming back to our quarterdeck. After that "James" became our nickname for the submerged robot.

Hi-tech equipment littered the boat, diving gear dripped, our luxury yacht indeed looked like something from a spy movie and I was the "temporary owner".

We were searching for the wreckage of a sunken luxury cruise boat valued, according to the Lloyd's representative on board with us, to be over seven hundred and fifty thousand dollars. It was said to have been pirated, then torched, somewhere along the Corfus coastline.

I found myself elevated from first mate to "owner" of the vessel for duration of this operation.

This safari was looking up. What had started out as a quick crewing job was turning into a dinkum, deep-sea treasure hunt!

We had been testing the boat, before potential buyers showed up to make an offer, when we got wind of the maritime rhubarb.

The previous evening, a Cambridge accent at the other end of the taverna, was trying to get a point across to Hellenic port police and was being drowned by a local fishermen and a couple of file-wielding officials.

From what I could gather, the fisherman, who claimed the largest vessel in Corfus bay, was adamant that his canted-deck boat could accommodate the wetsuits and their electronic paraphernalia.

Lloyd's was concerned about the weather—February in the Med is unpredictable and, he also pointed out, the equipment was worth more than the boat.

Below deck facilities were also a requirement.

The Coast Guard only had a Zodiac in the vicinity and Lloyds would have had to foot the bill a uniform explained.

"Freedom C, would be perfect for them," I said to Günter, whose boat it was that we had come to flog. It was spacious and opulently equipped.

Corfus itself is a rather remote, little village on the Peloponnesian coastline and had little to offer in the way of ocean going vessels.

Günter told me that if I brokered the deal he would cut me in for a third of the charter. He suggested it be best if I appear to be the owner of the yacht and he my Captain. This would then naturally explain who controlled the helm during salvage operations.

"Vot vill I say to Lilly?" asked Günter. Lilly his wife, had made me promise that we would "behave", concerned perhaps that the lure of distant ports would get us into troubled waters.

"Tell her the truth, she'll understand the delay," I suggested.

Günter decided to wait and see.

Mr. Lloyds loved the proposal and we agreed upon a decent daily rate, plus a handsome bonus if it was proved that arson was the cause.

"If this can find keys still stuck in the ignition on the fly bridge for instance," he pointed to the mini-sub's aluminum trunk, "then we would have a case and you would be entitled to a percentage of the insurance value."

"Done," said I. "This is Captain Günter—"

They had seven days in which to find the wreck or call the search off.

A deep, jagged coastline surrounds Corfus bay and is only a three-hour sail out of Piraeus, hence it being a favourite place with local scuttlers. Law dictates that the Greek port police authorize and accompany any such underwater investigation to prevent submerged historical relics being nabbed; so a dozen badges clambered on board when we left shortly after first light.

The little, remote-controlled, yellow submarine was amazing. Camera angle, zoom and adjustable lights, at depths well below normal scuba. A couple of false alarms had the English and Greek divers bailing overboard to investigate old keels.

Fish and plummeting seascapes were scanned all day.

"And ve have James Bond the mini submarine, some divers, police and a man from Lloyds," said Günter, explaining into the mouthpiece on the tavernas' only phone that night.

"I don't know how long, maybe ve find it tomorrow—but no longer than a veek."

"She vants to speak to you," he said, thrusting the hand piece at me.

I confirmed that yes, we did have a submarine called James on board and we were working for Lloyds of London on a piracy case.

Lilly wanted to know if we'd been drinking.

"I told you she vouldn't believe us," said my Captain.

The novelty had worn thin by the third day and the crew dwindled to a skeleton. But "James" suddenly found some solid evidence of a recently sunken luxury boat in the evening, satellite coms debris, railings and batteries. However, it was getting late, so we simply marked the spot.

Lilly was on the dockside when we returned, having taken a various selection of transport modes, terminating in a long taxi ride to get there. She had decided to see for herself. She was most impressed and I dare say relieved to find that "James" really existed.

It took another day to ascertain that most of the wreckage had slid down to uneconomic depths. Only a very expensive salvage operation could recover further evidence, but the footage they had taped, might be sufficient for a conviction once they reviewed it under closer inspection back at the lab.

"We will let you know if we're successful," said Lloyds as he and "James" got in a truck and waved.

"Vere are the vages?" Günter grinned, knowing full well that I had nothing in writing.

"It'll depend on the result, they know where we live and will post us something according to the review."

"Uh-huh—I suppose it was worth it, just for the adventure and experience," he sounded sceptical, "it wos vinter and ve ver here anyway."

Freedom C was sold the following day.

The next season Günter and Lilly opened a restaurant on Hydra and it became a fairly regular hang out.

One lunch I asked for the *log* (short for logarismo—bill) and when he came out with my change, Günter shoved a huge wadge of drachmas into my hand.

"Your change, Sir," he said, trying to keep a poker face.

It took a second—months had passed since the "James" encounter.

"You mean wages Captain—the double-O department coughed up, right?"

"Ja, a surprise for all of us at the Post Office this morning, I had nearly forgotten."

Memories of our final voyage on Freedom C were made even more enjoyable.

Sometimes I would give Lilly and Günter a hand in "The Moita Restaurant", named after another vessel Günter had previously owned.

"There are sixteen Norwegian guys here off a yacht. Their boss turns fifty tomorrow and they want a party here," Günter explained. "These guys drink a lot, so I need help on the bar and with orders."

The jovial band of "Scandahooligan's", had "hej-hoed" their way through a few toasts by the time the Caesar Salad was served.

"Excuse me, sir," an arm beckoned, "there is something in my salad."

The table pretended not to notice as I went over. The largest, blackest, slimiest slug imaginable writhed on the lettuce.

Had I not spent over a decade examining local fauna and flora, I might have been caught, but I knew no such beast could be native.

I decided not to give their prank away and called Lilly over. Petite in every way is a word that accurately describes her.

She squealed in surprise. The Norwegians continued to look appropriately shocked at the slithering garnish, hej-grumbling, one pointing to the bougainvillea above the table.

Günter sauntered over—

"Fokkin'-shit, I'm sorry gentlemen, did you vant that grilled?" he asked, turning to go. "I vill get the chef."

Willy was then hauled from the galley to inspect the dish and looked in disbelief. He had worked his way up through the kitchens of Amsterdam and returned to Greece now experienced enough to handle a commercial galley. His re-appearance had coincided with Günter's new restaurant.

"But I washed the lettuce," he squawked, which was met with guffaws from the yachtsmen no longer able to contain their prank.

Günter wanted to keep the giant slug—his motives mysterious.

Turned out that this was a seafaring, jet set slug and not for sale.

"No, no we take him to Spetses tomorrow. This slug has traveled half way around the world with us and only once did we get offered a meal—but of course we paid!"

"But you guys handled it the best so far," chuckled their blond, bearded, leader. "We insist on buying you a drink—"

I asked Günter what he had intended doing with the giant, black slug.

"Pickling it of course," he said, his eyes glinting over gold-framed glasses. "And putting it in someone's cocktail."

Günter spent a lot of time, behind the bar thumbing fancy yacht magazines for a season or two, reminiscing and window-shopping well beyond the restaurant's income capability.

The Beard's Bullion

Once upon a time the island was rich—very rich.

Its citizens had struck a deal with the ruling Ottomans, whereby if they donated their first-born sons to the Sultan's fleet, they would in return be given license to trade freely.

As a result the Hydriotes plied the Mediterranean, unhindered by the occupying Turkish Empire, accumulating wealth and power.

To this day the captains' spectacular, stone mansions adorn the amphitheatre that overlooks the little harbour as evidence of their success.

According to island legend and in the absence of a national banking system, inhabitants of the time were prone to hiding their wealth in the *cisternas* (fresh water tanks) of their houses.

The Orthodox Church in Greece enjoyed vast prosperity and one local Hydriot priest, Baba Jannis, was said to have hoarded several hundred Louis XVI gold sovereigns. In current value it would exceed a million Sterling.

Even today the church carries considerable clout in the community. Citizens can be seen genuflecting and kissing the hands of long-bearded men in black on the streets. Distinctive, authoritative clerical figures, with stovepipe hats concealing manes of unshorn hair who waft to the front of queues in banks and post offices.

When the "old beard" passed on, his fortune never surfaced. It was rumoured that the treasure was still buried somewhere in the grounds of his vestry. Today a grand manor occupies this site owned by a retired English diplomat and his wife. The original church still stands adjacent to it.

"I'm going to Switzerland next week and I'll pick up an auger as we seem to have exhausted all the islands alternative mining tools," said Rob.

An auger I soon found out was a ferocious looking, rock-munching device that tunnels.

I looked at the paraphernalia we had accumulated in our excavation. Everything from the house vacuum cleaner to sharpened fence posts; even a pneumatic "Kanga" was proving to be too puny. The island isn't nicknamed the Rock for nothing. I had to agree, we definitely needed a more robust tool if our dig was to proceed. We went inside to discuss our options.

It is the nature of any small society to gossip and we were only too aware of the ridicule we could get if the word got out that the distinguished gent and myself were looking for buried bullion.

Rob had initially hired an Albanian fellow to assist with the manual labour under the guise of dealing with an encroaching root system that had gotten into the foundations of the house.

"There doesn't appear to be anything of an intrusive nature here Keerios?" said the help. Rob felt it prudent to let the fellow go rather than have to let him in on his wild scheme. That combined with the fact that he would quite possibly be throwing hard-earned pension money into a bottomless pit—literally.

Rob and Audrey were of the new-age ilk. Convinced not only that their house was planted on top of hidden gold but also that it was constructed on ancient lay-lines. Invisible energy lines, which had healing powers and good karma.

They had completely renovated the mansion upon purchase but at the time had not come across the original priest's cisterna. Nor were they aware of the mythical coins until years later.

They had reached a point in life where they were contemplating selling their home and moving back to England. The house being situated near the top of the town's steep hill, the climb had become less endearing as time passed. Convinced that the lost gold should be investigated before they sold off—they had consulted the Ouija board.

There was, according to the departed spirits, a fortune lying underneath the back courtyard. Backed up by a definite downward thrust of a divining rod, there appeared to be a lot of supernatural evidence supporting the theory of hidden treasure.

The fact that the courtyard was enclosed and out of sight, meant that the dig could be done in secret. I had known the Browning's for over a decade and they knew me to be a man who could keep his own council—

Rob had meticulously recorded the cryptic Ouija board conversations that Audrey had had with the departed beard most nights. He'd drawn up plans, made measurements and come up with an assessment worth investigating.

If I would throw in my lot and some muscle they would cut me in for a third of the treasure. I was fully aware, that despite the huge house, they lived on a retired diplomatic pension and were not able to justify the going rate for manual labour on a long shot.

I had nothing to loose, apart from a little sweat, by participating in this venture. In fact, I found the prospect of our treasure hunt exciting. I knew the island and its history well enough to know that the Hydriotes of old had squirreled their savings in obscure places. The bottom of a water-filled cisterna was a known favourite.

Upon my arrival each morning we would sit down to discuss what the Ouija board had said the night before. Rob had leaflets from Geneva coin collectors that gave the value of sovereigns. He had drawn up progress graphs and the angles of our dig. We would ponder the next few feet.

Audrey would periodically appear with chilled musta; a local version of non-alcoholic grape juice to quench our thirst and replace our body fluids. We would hack and chop at the tunnel face. With each change in shale texture we would inspect the bazi for signs of hope. Three meters down and under, we came across what appeared to be lime, which according to historical documents was an important ingredient in the construction of old water wells.

This gave us encouragement and the impetus to dig on. We would, on occasion flood the pit with water in an attempt to soften ground, which only created mud.

We would generally knock off before lunch and I would make my way down to the port only partially cleaned of the grime.

"A spot of gardening at the Browning's," I would say to the quizzical expressions on the harbour. Questions like "what are they planting, a forest?" were asked frequently.

I looked forward to my mornings on their front terrace, discussing and dreaming, sipping tea and musta in our shorts. Measuring, plotting, sharing an active morning with good company. Better than fishing, anyone could do that; we were digging for hidden treasure. It was a grand hobby.

We had a strong rumour, time, a historical location in an enclosed area, imagination and a sense of dare. Why not try; we had nothing to loose.

Eventually the excavated pile got so big it filled the back courtyard and anyone looking out of the kitchen window was bound, at the very least, to comment on the mine dump.

By this time, electric lighting had to be used at the face.

So we took the painful decision to fill it in and replaced the plakakia, vowing to re-open the tunnel, the following season.

We never did. Audrey needed a hip operation, Rob's joints wouldn't tolerate the strain, I opened an Internet shop in the port—life had moved on by the following season.

Sadly, the Browning's mansion is now for sale and they're slowly moving back to Blighty where the hills aren't quite so steep and cabs have wheels.

I wonder if the new owner would like to know the location of this dig?

We could possibly find an adventurous, young Irishman to man the auger.

A fitting end would be to mail a slice of the treasure cheque to the poltergeists who initiated the find, Mr. & Mrs. Ouija, c/o London, with thanks and vindication!

Spiders and Sleep

I returned to my bunker from dinner one night and taking off my jacket in the gloom before turning on the bedside lamp I noticed a black sock caught in the corner, six inches above the pillow.

The "sock" stood up when I switched on the main light.

Eight legs as long as my little finger.

Africa offers a larger variety of arachnids and other micro-terrors so I had had some experience in dealing with this type of invasion. I also know that rare species should be protected; nature conservation becomes second nature with some upbringings.

The spider didn't take much coaxing onto the end of a broom.

I awkwardly carried it outside and placed it under the lemon tree of Yaya Theodora from whom I rented a couple of rooms and a tiny outside ablution.

We had a most amicable accommodation arrangement. She would surprise me with the odd little kitchen treats; I would lend a periodic hand with the hammer.

She nurtured the little garden; I enjoyed fresh basil and lemons.

We respected each other's personal space, the perfect Yaya for a bachelor.

It was spring on the island. Flowers and buzzing were everywhere.

Also, I discovered, the Tarantula's had come out of hibernation and were beginning to stake out their summer hunting grounds.

Sharing a small room with a spider that large would have had a detrimental affect on sleep, Africa or no. My eight-legged friend could have the garden, indoors was for humans. Me.

Next morning, Yaya Theodora assured me that I had been very unlucky, as she had only seen two in all the years of living there. She lived in the other half of the small L-shaped cottage and had her own separate outside loo.

A crack in the wall above my bed had widened a centimetre during a previous seismological event and even though the spider was probably too big to have emerged through it, other crawlies could, so I moved the bed into the opposite corner of the room.

Almost to the day a year later, I returned one evening to find my hairy friend above the bed again, just a few inches from my pillow.

I got the broom, thinking that if this was the same spider, then he'd lost a lost of weight—and was a lot more agile!

It scuttled up the broom handle, which got dropped instantly.

Luckily the little blighter ran up the wall not under furniture and I was able to encourage it slowly back onto the broom.

Yaya told me it was probably the same one; it just hadn't had a substantial meal yet.

A couple nights later a juvenile, about two and a half inches in diameter, occupied the corner behind the television diagonally opposite the bed.

Scrunched paper was used to apprehend this arachnid and both were placed into the kitchen rubbish bag.

I lay in bed feeling guilty that I'd been a bit harsh on the little spider when the possibility dawned on me that it could chew its' way through the layer of plastic with its' fangs—and escape into the kitchenette.

I got up and tied a second bag over the rubbish.

No sooner was I horizontal, than I figured that if it could escape through one bag, then why not two.

Slumber would be easier knowing that the spider was outside.

Wrapped in a towel, I took the bag out to the shower where an escape wouldn't be drastic and the *skoopethia* (rubbish) would still be safe from the scavenging cats. The thinking was that I would carry it downhill in the morning.

One less "tarantoola" in the neighbourhood would surely reduce the odds of another of these "unusual" encounters. I dismissed the subject from mind.

After the late movie the following night, I had just switched off the light, when I heard and felt a plop on the bed next to me.

Had a small pebble fallen from the ceiling? That would have meant it would have fallen against the wall side, not on the pillow next to my head?

When I flipped on the bedside lamp, I was just in time to see four hairy legs disappear between the mattress and the wall. Further attempts to capture the little swine failed when it eight-legged-it underneath the bed frame.

Each sheet, blanket and pillow was gingerly inspected for the invader. Sympathy and "conservation-training" waned rapidly when the search progressed to shaking out every dusty old boot and shoe that was piled under the double bed.

Hunting spiders and moving furniture in the middle of the night, tends to discourage kip and encourage irritation. The heavy mattress was over turned, dusty suitcases dragged out and eventually the little bastard broke cover, scuttled for the door and was unceremoniously assisted outside by a swift sweep.

Worried that I might have damaged a leg I went outside to inspect.

"*Tee echies?*" asked Yaya Theodora, in her gown wanting to know what I was doing with a torch under the lemon tree in the early hours.

"Po-po-poe; another one?" she responded. "Most unusual."

She was equally perplexed as to why I hadn't stomped on it in the first place. "Next year we only have more—"

The following day I popped over to my neighbour's house where a couple of Syrian mates were renovating. There was a yelp from the garden as one of them had uncovered a juvenile, nestling under some leaves.

"Where we come from these things can kill you." Stomp.

I belatedly argued that the Hydra kind were comparatively docile and not known to be deadly. Also for some reason, they only seemed to inhabit one side of the hill, a limited colony.

I still wasn't convinced genocide was the way to go with endangered species.

This conviction however changed the next day.

After I had seated myself in the tiny outhouse, I had to bend slightly in the shower to avoid hitting roof beams and watch out for elbows when drying, I went to grab a roll.

Directly in front of my hand was the mother of all tarantulas.

Fat and hairy as a mouse, about to spawn several hundred offspring by the look—

The loo brush broke. I took solace in the fact that this killing had been in the interest of self-defence. I already had the jitters after only half a dozen territorial disputes; a new generation of them was too appalling to contemplate. Tarantulas are nocturnal hunters, so I had taken to automatically scouring the corners and ceilings upon entering the bunker at night and shaking sheets. Divisions of her brood would have had me on the street and such secure, comfortable, long-term bachelor digs were hard to come by.

It got worse.

A couple of days later, I was drying my back off after a cooling, midnight shower, when I felt what I thought was an olive twig or locust leg snagged in the towel. My little bathroom stood under an olive tree and bits blew in periodically between the tiles.

There was a quick, sharp pain in my left index finger.

As I pulled my hand from behind my back, I saw with horror that the daddy of all tarantulas was hanging off my fingertip. Hairy inches—multiple legs—splayed in the air.

I instinctively flicked and simultaneously banged my head on the beam, yelping.

The only decent armament, the loo brush, hadn't yet been replaced after my disagreement with mummy spider.

The perpetrator had vanished; so dazed and starkers I dashed into the garden in search of a club, light flooding out of the open door.

"*Ti echies?*" Yaya Theodora had come to investigate the commotion and hadn't quite comprehended the sight before her. I was sucking one index and covering with the other hand.

"*Pali Tarantoola.*" Another, I explained backing still unarmed into the loo.

The only weapon on hand now was the toilet bin or a toothbrush.

Upon lifting the metal disposer my adversary made a break for the back of the porcelain.

I missed with a noisy swipe and it dashed towards my dripping self.

I was then motivated to get really active with the dustbin.

All Yaya could hear was an unholy racket going on the tiny bathroom and her voice seemed concerned.

"*Eesa endaxi?*" Was I okay?

Had her tenant finally gone around the twist? Cavorting naked in the garden at midnight and now making enough noise to wake the dead. Other lights in the neighbourhood went on.

I eventually emerged wrapped and holding one of the eight limp legs.

"*Bravo-sou,*" said Yaya, applauding the dangle.

A week later, the inverted and curled corpse, was still lying beneath the olive tree so big the ants hadn't managed to move the exoskeleton

An Australian skipper and mate who had come to visit, was impressed when I showed him the evidence to go with two small puncture marks on my finger.

"*Bravo-sou,*" said Yaya for the umpteenth time as she passed, still happy that I had finally learned about the law of the jungle.

"It's your *spiti* (house) and you are the man."

It took this man some weeks, before he stopped shaking out shoes and towels. I still suspect that Yaya's magnified spectacles were always under prescribed—two in twenty years indeed!

Two Tonys and the Traumatic Trinket

Bill and I would usually spend St Patrick's Day preparing stew and practicing the art of making and sampling Irish coffee. Tony, the only other Paddy on the island, was a builder and part-time fisherman who lived in Vlichos, a little village down the coast. He had promised to bring some Guinness and had been due to arrive before the rest of the gang turned up that evening.

He hadn't showed by the time the party was in full swing, so I gave him a call, thinking it was unusual for my fellow countryman to be missing out on our national day. He sounded exhausted.

"I can't explain why now and you probably won't believe me when I tell you, but a funny thing happened," he said. "And it's certainly not something that I would try and describe over the phone—but when I do, you have got to promise me, you won't tell a soul."

He did get around to telling me some days later and as excuses go for missing a party, this one tops the list.

Tony had apparently been suffering from a dreadful cold that particular blustery day and had decided to spend it in bed gathering his resources for our St Patrick's bash.

"The wind was howling and the sea had gotten really rough, when I got a phone call from my neighbour, Jorgo, to say my boat was in danger of being smashed against the rocks and he advised me to drag it up the beach."

Tony went onto to describe how he had forced himself out from under the covers, dragged on his "wellie boots" and gone down to pull his boat out of harms way.

"It weighed a ton and in my weakened condition I only managed to shift it up a couple of meters."

He'd returned home, got undressed and climbed back into bed. No sooner had he settled when the phone rang again.

"Leatherboy this time, wanting to know if I had a hacksaw."

Leatherboy Tony was the only other expat resident of Vlichos, so nicknamed, not just to alleviate confusion between the two Tonys, but because of his affection for leather gear. In summer his black, leather shorts promenaded the harbour front. In winter he would exchange his "hozen" in favour of tight biking pants, a noticeable fellow in our small village. Leatherboy Tony and Irish Tony, it stopped muddling the two.

"Hi Tone, can I come around and borrow a little saw?"

Irish Tony had one of the best-equipped private workshops on the island. Leatherboy was a musician and cook, not usually prone to handyman stuff.

"Sure," Irish Tony had said. "But I am in bed with the flu, so just let yourself in and help yourself."

No sooner had Irish Tony nodded off, when the phone went again. Jorgo, to inform him that the waves had increased and that the boat still wasn't safe.

"So I got all dressed up again, this time with a coat because it had started raining too and managed to drag the boat up another couple of feet."

As if on cue when the Irishman had just been dozing off between the sheets, the phone rang again. This time Leatherboy's voice had a hint of distress in it, but Irish Tony was too off colour himself to take much notice.

"Err—I think I need a pair of pliers as well."

"Just come and take whatever you want," said Irish Tony, now beginning to loose patience with matters.

"I swear I had just nodded of when the bleedin' phone went again," he explained, "it was Jorgo, to tell me that the sea had gotten even rougher and that the waves were now crashing right up the beach."

Tony had dutifully donned his foul weather gear and gone out for a third time to secure his craft. By now it was the middle of the afternoon and the chances of a siesta before the party were looking slim, but he decided to try and catch a nap anyway.

"The frigging phone went again I tell you." This time Leatherboy's voice was emitting distinctly strained sounds.

"I can't do this by myself, I need help."

"What?"

"Well, err, it's a bit difficult to describe," squeaked Leatherboy. "It's awkward to explain, but I think I need to use your vice."

"What's the problem"?

"I'll have to show you," whined Leatherboy. "But you have got to promise that you will never tell anyone."

"Just tell me what the problem is."

"Well, I would go to a hospital, but what with this weather there are no ferries off the island—," Leatherboy added, to emphasize the level of crisis.

Intrigued, Irish Tony got dressed for the sixth time, went outside and down to the workshop.

"I saw Leatherboy, hobbling along the path to my house, he was very red in the face and looked to be in extreme pain."

I believe the device is called a cock-ring, something a man inserts over his penis to keep an erection and prolong organism. Leatherboy had apparently been experimenting with this gadget at home alone and found he couldn't get it off. The more he fiddled, the more the swelling increased and the more difficult it became to dislodge.

It wasn't the sort of predicament he wished to share. So he had limped over to Irish Tony's workshop and picked up a small hacksaw with the intent of cutting said metal tourniquet off.

The trouble was, that by the time he got home, the swelling had all but covered the gadget. Bent double and with shaking hands, he found the task impossible.

Still loath to share his plight, he figured that if he could grab the ring with a pair of pliers and saw carefully, he might solve the problem.

He had limped the half kilometre to the workshop and back, only to find the affliction had yet more increased in size and darkened in colour. Attempting to grasp the trinket by now proved to be beyond the limit of tolerance.

It had been some hours of ever increasing pain and he had felt that he was at serious risk of permanently loosing anatomical stuff. The prospect of a whole night in this condition was too horrible to contemplate.

"I'm not going to even tell you the condition he was in, poor bloke," said Irish Tony, shuddering at the memory. "You shoulda' seen his eyes when he saw I had the fever shakes making the hacksaw vibrate."

"So while you lot were having a grand ol' time, I was performing a delicate operation with some blokes penis in my workshop vice," said Irish Tony. "I missed the party but I tell you something, it won't be a St Paddy's I'll forget in a hurry."

Nor apparently will Leatherboy, who can still sport his shorts with pride, on whatever island he migrated to.

Peter the Painter

"You gotta help me man," said Peter, sounding more distraught than usual. "Boogie's dead!"

Peter the Painter, an American artist, spent most of his time trying to simplify life. The trouble was, the more he simplified it, the more complicated it became. He was not a man accustomed to timepieces, indeed calendars were not items he consulted either. It was well known that Peter and punctuality were not words to be used in the same breath.

He took island living to a slower level.

On my way over the hill, I pondered my friend's latest predicament. His charge had suddenly kicked the bucket under mysterious circumstances.

He certainly seemed to be having a run of bad luck.

Only the day before he had called me from Athens wanting to know the DEH (electricity office) phone number.

"Do you think the National Electric Company of Greece, can switch individual apartments off?"

I told him I doubted it and wanted to know why.

He explained that he had decided to escape the island and take up an offer from a mutual acquaintance to stay in her swish Kolonaki apartment while she was away.

Just as the early morning hydrofoil was pulling out of the harbour, he had remembered that in his haste to make it, he had forgotten to turn the electric stove off and was concerned about combustibility.

I inquired as to alternative means of gaining access to his flat.

"Only the landlord has a spare set of keys but the house is a mess," he said. "Plus, I don't want him to know I'm a fire hazard."

He decided that the best thing to do was to cut short his stay in the "Big Olive" and return to the island on the next dolphin, the first of which was early the next day. Stressing under the worry about his abode but figuring that there was little else he could do about the situation, he picked up a few vital art supplies and took himself to dinner.

Peter was a good-looking bloke who was not known for discarding flirtational opportunities. Not least when on parole in the big city.

This meant a late night had followed.

It was shortly before dawn when he nodded off, having brought a friend back to the flat for a nightcap, so he overslept and hadn't heard the alarm.

"First thing I knew was the phone ringing and someone saying that there was a taxi waiting outside the apartment. I only had half-an-hour to make the hydrofoil."

It being out of season, there were only two dolphins a day, one early morning and one late afternoon. He dared not miss the early one; smouldering ruins were beginning to haunt his imagination.

He had just made the hydrofoil and was settling back in his seat mulling over the chaos that had been the trip, when an awful thought dawned on him. In his haste to flee, he had scrunched up the sheets, emptied the ashtrays and generally squared the flat away as best he could in the forty-five seconds before legging it for the waiting cab.

"I was feeling a little slothful for not properly tidying up my hostess's apartment, when it suddenly struck me," Peter said, "the condom—the used condom was still lying on the floor, beside the bed on the opposite side to the door!"

He had followed instructions and had left the keys inside the apartment on the kitchen table before pulling the Yale lock front door behind him. There seemed to be no way the evidence could be cleared up before the owner got back.

It would be with much embarrassment, that he would have to explain the item in question, perhaps over a nice dinner?

He was still stewing over this pickle, when he got off the boat and was immediately accosted by a lady in need of help.

Damsels in distress were Peter's specialty and with his guard already lowered he accepted the mission.

"Ahh Pedro, just the man I wanted to see."

Lena, his pretty neighbour was about to board the same boat on its way back to Athens and had asked Peter if he wouldn't mind dog sitting for a couple of days.

All he had to do was pop over in the morning, throw some food in a bowl and let the doggie have a run around the terrace, before locking it inside for the night.

It sounded simple enough. The mutt was called Boogie, a highly pedigreed miniature Yorkshire terrier, no bigger than some sewer rats and shouldn't pose much of a problem he was assured.

"Thank you Pedro, you saved my life," expressed Lena. "Here are the keys to the flat and there's dog food in the fridge."

I arrived to find Peter pacing the terrace in a state of distress. He pointed to an ominous six-inch stain on the tiles outside his front door.

"A Boogie-stain man. I've scrubbed with detergent, chlorine, hot water and it still won't disappear."

"What happened," I asked. "How did a perfectly healthy, young dog die within twenty-four hours of your care?"

"I don't know," he moaned. "I got up, fed the dog and let it out on the terrace while I popped down to Four Corners to get some coffee. When I came back there he was. I couldn't have been gone ten minutes and I returned to see this ball of fluff lying just there in a dark puddle—pink tongue hanging out."

Lena's terrace was situated above Peter's house so the little dog must have fallen the height of a full story and died instantly.

"There's been a large, grey cat loitering about the neighbourhood—maybe it chased Boogie. Mind you, some leap for the mutt to have cleared the wall, I didn't know they could jump that high."

"What did you do with the corpse?" I inquired.

"Well, I didn't know whether Lena would like to bury the pet herself and I didn't want it attracting flies, so I put it in her freezer."

The look on my face prompted him to add quickly, "I did wrap it in a plastic bag so it wouldn't contaminate the food."

"What am I going to say to Lena, she loved that mutt?"

He had no contact number for Lena and decided that the only thing to do was inform her friend in the hope that the news could be broken gently to her before she got up the hill. Visions of her opening the fridge and finding a frozen dog were appalling.

"She'll freak out," said Peter. "I toyed with the idea of leaving a warning note on the freezer door but that seemed even more bizarre. I just hope we can catch her before she heads home."

We were still pondering the burial of a frozen dog on our way down to the port when Iris spotted us.

"Ahh Pedro, just the man I wanted to see," said Iris, with her geriatric, blind mongrel in tow.

"I have to go to Athens and I was wondering if you wouldn't mind looking after Fluffy for a few days?"

With the look of incredulity on my friends face I couldn't help but guffaw and quickly apologized to Iris, who must have thought my response rude.

"Trust me Iris, Peter is out of the dog sitting, key holding business for a while."

Peter has returned to the First World, but nobody predicts he won't be back.

Donkey Walkabout

Putting along the coast peering with binoculars I was at my wits end. How could such a large animal have vanished?

Particularly a high-profile donkey like Dardo!

Three days with everyone on the island looking out for him and still no sign of the blighter.

I had discovered a broken tether rope when I went to feed him in the morning and as he rarely wandered far had scouted the immediate area. Normally he responded heartily to the call for breakfast.

My second port of call was down to Four Corners, where he had been known to *klepsy* (steal) the vegetables on display. A favourite habit of runaway donkeys I had already discovered.

"Oxi," Dimitri tutted, "I would have noticed the thief."

Dimitri's shop stood on an important junction on the Kamini to Hydra road and most traffic, mule or man, was observed. A large unattended appetite would certainly have been noted.

I extended my search spreading the word further a field.

The port, other vegetable grocers, Kamini and the Muleteer Union—but nothing. Nobody had seen Dardo.

Considering this was a community that knew exactly which cat belonged to whom and where they lived, the loss a very distinctive donkey was extraordinary.

A Cypriot donkey is a breed as large as a mule; Dardo was retired and had a conspicuous grey coat and big head. He would infiltrate port-front tavernas to nuzzle for bread—everyone knew Dardo.

I had come to the conclusion that someone had borrowed him or was playing a prank and gave up looking at sunset.

By the second morning he still hadn't turned up.

The police put out an APB and further spots were investigated.

Mandraki Bay to Palametha.

It was established that Dardo hadn't been seen boarding a fishing boat, hydrofoil, ferry or water taxi, which meant he was definitely still on the Rock.

By day three, I took up the offer to motor around the island on a mate's ciaqui as by then the vanishing of Dardo, had become an island mystery that had to be solved.

It was getting late and we were headed back to the harbour, when I saw a long shadow behind a shrub in an open patch of land, adjacent to an old mansion, smack between Kamini and the port. I noted the spot.

The loudest hee-haw you can imagine greeted me, big ears up.

Dardo had been grazing randomly and managed to wrap the dragging rope around the base of a bush a few of times.

Eventually, the rope became so short he was harnessed right up against a well-nibbled shrub, a mere couple of hundred meters from home.

"Ahh, you found him," chortled Felix, from his usual chair as Dardo and I passed by the "Three Brothers" next day.

"Gone walk about had he?"

"No, actually Felix, I went walkabout, he went standabout!"

Dead-ication to Art

"Yuk, what's that stink?" said Elizabeth, an aspiring New York artist, stopping in her tracks.

I recognized the whiff; something deceased and I was keen to head back in the opposite direction.

"Nothing you want to know about, let's check out the other side."

The two of us had been exploring an uninhabited, little island off the coast of the Peloponnese.

We had anchored in the crystal waters of a secluded bay and had rowed a dingy to shore.

"Zoë Zoë", was a magnificent twin-masted wooden sloop, captained by an Australian friend and long time expatriate of Hydra.

He had extensively sailed the Aegean for three decades and knew exactly where to find "undiscovered" coves, private anchorages being our preference.

Elizabeth and I had rowed the inflatable tender ashore and spent the morning clambering around the island. One old, stone hut ruin the only indication of any former human habitation with a few wild rabbit and goat droppings the only evidence of current life.

She had opted to spend her sabbatical year working on Hydra, an island known to attract artists. She was focused on art but had a tendency to be scattered about other matters in life. Thus acquiring the affectionate nickname of the "Noodle".

I had invited her to join us on an end of season cruise. A last run before permanent winter mooring and we had spent an enjoyable couple of days sailing the Greek waters in perfect autumn weather.

Undeterred, the Noodle insisted on investigating the smell and walked over to the precipice.

At the bottom of a small cliff lay a semi-decomposed ram.

It must have lost its footing and plunged into the ravine. Once a handsome beast with splendid corkscrew horns, now the brown and white skin was drawn taught revealing white ribs.

"Oooh," crowed Elizabeth, surveying the ex-goat. "That's just what I've been looking for."

This from a smidge of a lass who collected sick kitties and saved ants.

I thought she was joking.

"You're kidding right?" Most young ladies would have gagged at the sight.

"What on earth do you want with a decaying corpse?"

"To sculpt—come on let's find a way down—I need that skull."

The fact that it was still attached to the decomposed body didn't seem to have crossed her mind.

The previous evening we had pulled in to a little fishing village and the Noodle had spotted some exotic, brightly coloured fish in the market.

"I need a selection of those to paint when we get back," she announced. "I want that blue one, a couple of those reds and that—"

The Captain had pointed out that we still had a couple of days a sea. The stench of aging fish in the confined quarters of the sloop might not be such a good idea.

"What if I wrap them in double plastic and put them in the fridge." Freezing was not an option in our galley.

This compromise was reluctantly agreed to.

Smells have a way of permeating everything and every time we went to the galley icebox, a waft of fish market managed to infiltrate the cabin, poli-plastic bags not withstanding. It had already attracted commentary from the crew. Going to ask the skipper if my guest could bring a rotting skull on board as well seemed to be pushing it.

"I'm going to need a sharp knife to cut its' head off and carve some of the dead skin away. Will you go back to the boat and get one—and maybe some pliers," she bubbled, happily. "I've always wanted to do a ram's head sculpture, what a find!"

The yacht's klaxon sounded lunch while I was swimming back to the sloop having left the tender for her and the trophy.

"You'll never guess what the Noodle wants to do now," I said. The first mate was putting the final touches to lunch. Frying sausages and eggs disguising the smell of fish in the galley.

"I need to borrow that knife when you're finished."

"Absolutely not." The Captain and mate didn't have the stomach for it either.

I swam back to shore and delivered the captain's ruling.

"But I'll pick it clean," said the Noodle, who by this time had managed decapitation and was down at the waters edge. "I'll wash it off in sea water, so they won't smell a thing."

"Well, you go back and negotiate with the skipper," I said jokingly, not wishing to jeopardize my berth on the vessel.

She did and won, on the proviso that the skull would be odourless.

But even with scrubbing and picking skeletons manage to keep some pong.

"Only when you put your nose up close," implored the Noodle, when she returned with her prize later.

Trouble was we didn't have plastic bags big enough to fit the head but once on board she wasn't going surrender her prize.

There was no denying her dead-ication to art and such enthusiasm had to be commended and accommodated.

I came up with a plan that seemed to satisfy the crew.

"Let's attach it to a rope and dangle it in the water off the stern."

That evening, we moored in another small bay with a couple of other yachts. The sailing community is a friendly bunch and we invited a family over for cocktails just as it was getting dark.

There was a sudden piercing shriek from the deck above followed by a large splash. Our guest's ten-year-old daughter had decided to investigate the rope hanging off the back of the sloop.

An ashen-faced kid appeared in the hatchway.

"What were you using for bait?" she squeaked.

Routers & E-Rhubarbs

Living on a small island, one is out of mainstream society, particularly in a foreign country where language and communications are prohibitive. One gets left behind.

In '96 when I was visiting some friends in Sweden, my first time abroad in years, I "discovered" the Internet. The fourteen-year-old son of my host had a full colour monitor—a novelty—and a computer that could perform magic. I have always been a gadget fan and was drawn to the kid's bedroom attracted by the amazing audiovisual graphics on a game he was playing.

He gave me a demonstration of what it could do, including digital photos and sophisticated word processing programs. Up until then, the most advanced machine I'd worked on was an "antique" Apricot. For those who don't remember, it was an early competition to the first Apple PC's, back at the beginning of the '80's. It weighed two tons, was mouse-less and had a curved, green screen.

Windows '95 appeared to be much more user friendly. It played music and one could create just about anything on paper.

"Plus you can download stuff off the Internet," the lad quipped, amazed at my blank expression.

"You know—Email?" I hadn't a clue.

I did have a business card with a mate's details. He had been waffling on about computerized coms that summer on his annual holiday from Canada but it hadn't meant a thing to me.

My introducee informed me that there was an e-address on the card apparently, something with an @ in it, was the clue.

"Let's send him one, it costs nothing."

"For the price of a local phone call and you can send dozens," he continued explaining. I couldn't imagine communicating with Ottawa for under the price of a stamp. We got a reply within minutes.

I was hooked there was nothing like this on the island and I sensed this was my answer to changing my way of living. After a dozen years of being a jack of all, the time and age had come—to get behind a desk again.

All one needed was a computer, electricity and a phone line apparently.

I double-checked these simple facts. The island had electricity, I had a phone (I had waited nearly five years for the line though) and I could devise a way of obtaining a computer, my wallet not instantly extending that far.

When I returned to Greece, I already had it in mind to create a "digital-telex-office" and to build an "information magazine" about the island. A room on the port for emailing, a place for advertisers, real estate and news with printable discount coupons for participants—an amalgamation of my pre-island skills!

A friend was coming to live in full time on Hydra, having given up on Scandinavian winters. He needed something to do in his semi-retirement on the Rock and liked the idea. He was just out of first world commerce and I assumed was clued up in the techno basics of the mid '90s.

Because I was burbling about what could be done on the Internet he assumed I was fairly proficient.

So we went into Athens to see about a provider and equipment costs.

"Twelve to fifteen thousand dollars." And this was just for the connection. In Greece at that time, dollars were often quoted when talking in large amounts. It sounded less than asking for tens of millions of drachmas.

But, I'd been assured that with three basic ingredients I could have coms in the Himalayan hinterland. Routers and cost per meter didn't come into it.

No way was my partner going to foist that amount of capital into bringing the Net to the island.

I assured him it could be done, if Mongolians had access then so could we. We invested in a couple of PC's, a scanner and printer. Eventually a less expensive way to hook up to Athens was found.

As I didn't want to show my partner how much of an amateur I was in techno-logistics, I didn't leap into the boxes as soon as we hauled them back to the island and into our little office. He too, agreed we should paint the place out and build some basic furniture before un-packing.

Little did I know, he was just as nervous about unpacking for similar reasons as he hadn't gone on-line yet either.

We eventually plugged and played, learning by trial and error.

Thus we opened the first "Internet cyber promotions" office, a couple of years before its time by island pace. The compromise was that we had to make a long distance call to get onto the web, which was a lot more than the projected local call cost.

We got around that by only going on for short calls to check mail and if anyone wanted to surf, they could cover the long distance phone charge to Athens.

My impressions of the World Wide Web were probably doubly accentuated by the fact that this technology had come to me out of the blue. Without the presence of curtain raising media, it came as a complete surprise.

When I had moved to the island, vinyl and cassette were the only forms of household music on tap. One day in '88, a bloke from LA came on vacation and unpacked a CD. I remember being amazed at the technology leap. A small round mirror and lasers, great sound and I still hadn't even heard of the technology.

The World Wide Web had even greater impact.

Initially, not everyone received this wondrous new communications system with open arms. Change always meets some opposition, indeed I had balked at "progress" on the island myself, but this felt inevitable and pioneering, it was a logical step for me to take.

Mates, some travelled expats not just locals, considered e-mailing a gimmick.

Nothing could beat a fax, we were told. It was just a con to get people to buy computers, a fad that would pass. For the kids.

Islanders really do have a speed of their own. It's one of the nice things about living here—if a little frustrating at times.

But enough people and passing tourists justified keeping the "HydraNet" shop alive and coms technology changed so fast that we were soon vindicated.

I got a real kick shortly after opening, being able to send photographs of a wedding to Sydney and New York simultaneously, within minutes of the event.

I slowly got the hang of it and attitudes changed.

To me, this ability to communicate for very little cost, where the world's biggest library was at one's finger tips on an island, which didn't cater for avid English readers, was as powerful as any invention I could think of.

Up there—with wheels and fire!

I guess the novelty started to wear thin when it became apparent that email was also a vehicle for idle natter and "ers".

The technology began to catch-up. Within the year a small branch of another new provider opened on a neighbouring island. One with the same dialup code so the cost of surfing dropped dramatically!

There was no hunting line for the five numbers provided and because the island was still on antiquated, analogue phone lines we were lucky to get connected at 10,000bps, super slow in current techno-terms.

No two numbers were in sequence and were more often then not engaged. Basic, by today's standards. Lines barely held signal some days and disconnection was frequent. Downloading always a gamble.

I was assured of an immanent switch to digital phone lines and that they would make all the difference to e-coms.

"Before the millennium for sure," was the same response to my question every few weeks. Three years later, a few hours shy of countdown, it eventually happened but by then the net had become a digital quagmire. Even on the island the novelty had worn thin.

Digital Dave

I knew the island was starting to understand what my little shop actually did, about two years into the operation, when some local sought me out on the port at night the day after Princess Di's death.

"Keerios David, we want to send a photograph to England—*tora*! (now)," a moustache enquired. "Your machine can do this we hear?"

My posted office hours were 10:00-14:30, six days a week and rarely were those hours fully occupied, so a special request at night, particularly from a local was novel.

For a couple of seasons I had tried to introduce the concept of the Internet to this small island community, which was still for the most part struggling with the introduction of electronic cash registers.

Indeed computers were much regarded with suspicion and associated either with some form of tax tracking device or were for kiddies' video games.

The island knew that Princess Di had spent some time on the Rock the week before her death and prided itself in the fact that she wasn't hounded by the Paparazzi during her visit. Dignitaries and the famous are not foreign to island inhabitants and privacy etiquette is respected throughout the community.

But upon her demise, wind of good dollars for last known photos of her, had filtered onto the port and a second rate candid shot taken from a semi-secluded vantage had surfaced.

The use of this picture for cash was the cause of much moral debate at the time.

But, it was an opportunity to show what Internet connections could do.

Yia ta mellon (the future) technology shown off at last and my kudus as a service soared.

The fact that the photo did eventually appear in the press was irrelevant; the moustaches had seen proof the net worked.

But it wasn't until some months later, when I sold a house via the Internet, that local punters really came over the fence.

Fishermen and muleteers all suddenly had *spiti's* (houses) for sale. Often at hugely inflated prices! The reason was because, not only had my "gimmick" lobbied a sale right near the heart of town but my customers, these blokes with computers, were prepared to go to financial war and pay even more than the asking price. Unheard of in local land trading, usually one haggled down.

So my first and only true sale via the Internet made island headline news. A house sale, that seemed fairly priced at forty-five-million Drachmas but hadn't had a nibble in four years, suddenly erupted into a face saving, last minute auction in which my guy won, paying the seller an extra eight million—and involved an unprecedented amount of actual legwork.

I learned a very valuable lesson during the sale of this house, never consider a deal done, not even if all parties shake hands on it in front of a lawyer, until the paperwork is signed. Especially on a Friday afternoon!

"See you all back here in my office first thing Monday morning," I had said, after everyone shook hands. Jenny the lawyer, would complete the legal documentation over the weekend, keys and autographs would be handed over then too.

My guy went off to pop the champagne.

According to cricket we had won, the fact that cricket isn't a known sport here, hadn't dawned on me.

"She wants more money," said my guy, in a tizz at 7.30am on Saturday. "She says she got an offer from a German for half a million more."

This was back in the days before mobile phones.

Negotiating between parties whose daytime destinations stretched from Vlichos to Mandraki, represented miles of walking.

My guy was of royal, Dutch ancestry but born and reared in the Far East, so he was accustomed to a saving face culture.

The German it transpired, was an editor and close buddy of a wealthy contingent of arty publishing types, who had already accumulated property on that side of the hill.

As the weekend progressed, the island's French expatriocracy allied itself with incoming Flemish/Thai blue blood, as did the Russians.

In short everyone got involved.

The outgoing resident Alexandra, an artist, had two small kids to support and naturally rooted for both sides. She was the chief spokes person for the family. A brother in New York and a sister holidaying on the island who were equal inheritors and added to the negotiating equation.

The trouble was that all through the bidding, myself representing the bloke from Bali, the rallied German troupe and the consenting brother and sister all had to be included step-by-step in the unexpected continuing negotiations. The furthest sunbathing beaches from town seemed to be the "venue de choice" for bartering.

Having gathered both sisters, the office phone was used to persuade the New York brother to take another offer from my guy.

More "deuts marken" would then enter the fray and the process would be repeated.

A point is reached where long-term real estate futures out weigh the current value being paid—a ceiling—and by then there was a lot of other involvement, so complete piracy was out of the question. Another property would have been hoisted before that happened, live punters get snapped up or chased away.

It was reported that burly Serge, my Russian mate, had acted as runner between two tavernas in Kamini on Saturday night, bolstering flagging Bali moral and translating.

There was no questioning the authenticity of the opposition, the new German editor, was a personal mate of long-time and respected homeowners of Hydra. A substantial chunk of the hill!

There was a serious risk of pissing both sides off with the escalation of price and community involvement and sending the deal south. Getting the sellers to agree amongst themselves was a feat in itself.

Multi-lateral rhubarbs had developed.

Half an hour before my bloke left on the Monday mid-morning dolphin, a parting "take-it-or-leave-it-shot", had been accepted.

Hydrofoil tickets were altered and my man bought the quaint little house that he has since upgraded into a villa of some opulence.

However, my taste for the real estate business had been quenched; it wasn't a game for cricketers.

It worked though, serious trading could be achieved, but I hadn't anticipated how far one would have to walk with this new information technology.

Digital Dave, stuck as a nickname for a couple of seasons, but the future caught up and I moved on.

Law and Disorder

Nobody else appeared to notice the chaos. To them this was normal. These throngs of legal cell phones and clutched files, interspersed by gesticulating, often unwashed clients of dubious income all of whom believe in the freedom to exercise vocal rights. Amongst these, the animated and the chain-smoking inhabitants of Greece's largest criminal court, I felt like the *alien* that I was by status. It tickled a few expats being documented as being alien on their visas.

It takes permanent island dwellers a bit of time adjusting to traffic and city bustle, when visiting the "Big Olive" after an extended period on the Rock. Being in a crowded Supreme Court for the first time was doubly intimidating.

Thirty-eight hours earlier I had been fairly relaxed, assured by my "suit" that this was a cut-and-dry case. The plaintiff, an heiress, was supposedly out of the country and wouldn't be in court.

She had met a cowboy and had taken to raising steers in Arizona. Our case was trivial in comparison to her usual shenanigans in front of the wigs, he had assured me. It certainly didn't merit the travel time and expense from her angle.

"Shut and open case, no problem," repeated my lawyer.

But then he had called the night before trail to inform me that I would have to take the stand after all. He wanted to know if my Greek was good enough to plead my version against the complaint.

A disturbing telephone call that had me awake with worry.

Doubts began to creep. I barely scraped by in island pigeon, judicial Greek was way above my understanding—and in Greece one is guilty until proved innocent!

I looked for the positives, surely I was in the clear having just the previous day managed to assemble a legally binding document from an elusive witness and friend of the Nemessee, assuring my innocence. An affidavit proving that somebody else had occupied the scene of the crime after my departure.

I had accepted kind advice and help from a peer, to ensure I had a lawyer in order to wave documents and guarantee my freedom.

What then was this new rhubarb I had enquired of my "suit".

It was apparent that with the cowgirl absent, the judicial system would still be quite keen on being reimbursed for the four years of work it had taken them to set a court date.

The matter of outstanding justice expenses hadn't occurred to me either. "Shut and open" took on a new meaning. Any contestant turning up could well be faced with footing the whole caboodle it seemed.

More distressing was the fact that my lawyer suddenly couldn't act as my translator.

Also, he wanted to know, could I muster any other dignitaries to testify on my behalf if things got rough? At this late stage!

I spent a couple of hours pretending sleep but without a wink.

I may have donned a jacket and tie but I was not sharp the next morning.

Fahgan Ntevint (Nt or nt in Greek, spells an English D) was the seventh criminal on the agenda list posted in the hall. Seventh, which according to instant sources, could be hours into the proceedings.

A louder bellow from the corner of the courtroom seemed to demand silence and the volume sank to a murmur-rhubarb.

The clock behind the pulpit said nine fifteen, only a quarter of an hour late. Punctual, by Hellenic clocks!

Stathis, my mate and moral support, had left with me for the Supreme Court in Piraeus with ample time in hand.

Time, which evaporated quickly, with regular stops to ask barely ambulant, geriatric gentlemen for directions; the only ones slow enough to catch in rush hour.

We were late but still on time if you know what I mean. Shy on sleep but not on caffeine, I twitched around the foyer as *numero ena* (number one) took the dock. The appearance of another staunch ally did much to bolster flagging reserves: although not officially in a position to do so, she said that she would take the stand to vouch for my integrity if necessary.

"Don't worry," she assured. "This is Greece, people go to court over the price of a loaf of bread."

The court was in the middle of the second case, about forty minutes into the proceedings, when Stathis announced that he was just popping out to extend the parking meter.

Case number three was a non-event; four, five and six were quickly executed or postponed.

"*Fahgan Ntevint numero epta.*" And my exalted witness was still out feeding the vehicle!

Panic and butterflies!

The lawyer gestured for me to come to the front of the courtroom.

Three Beaks glowered down on me, while my legal representative apologetically explained that my only witness was temporarily detained.

Tough looking birds. I flashed the lady judges what I hoped was my best "ignore-the-unkempt-hair-I'm-an-honest-joe" look.

The middle judge sternly interrupted my attorney's bid for time and blurted something directly at me.

"*Signo-me,*" I excused.

My lawyer quickly explained that I was a "*Xeni*" with limited Hellenic conversational skills. A word, which for some horrifying reason, caused a stir in the spectator arena and silence for the first time.

An alien was to be convicted—always a novelty.

I had waited four years to get to this point only to have my defence witness vanish. I imagined the court noting the delay as a sign of disrespect as we were told to remove ourselves.

Back to the smoky lobby until we had got our act together—more time to jitter.

By the time Stathis returned victim number eight was half convicted.

The time piece on the wall read 10.20am when my lawyer managed to jump back into the queue, in the process ousting a particularly vocal, balding, little fellow who was wielding a huge file.

Again there was that intimidating silence as the judge read the charges out loud. Interest seemed to intensify when it became apparent that the other side were also extraterrestrial, if absent.

My council quietly told me he wasn't going to produce my God-saving affidavit unless it was really necessary. Explaining that it only proved that the *klepsied* (missing) goods, (three sketches and half a dozen videos), could have vanished before I handed the keys over. My coveted written statement failed to mention whether the missing items were still in the house after I left.

Stathis took the stand but because he had translated the original police summons years before, was unacceptable as a witness and was dismissed. My mouth felt as though I'd been sucking dry chalk. Spiffing!

The Chief Wig beckoned me to the prisoners box and I suppose much like the composure that overcomes stage fright or when the whistle blows at the beginning of a rugby match, I stepped confidently forward, calm as a clam.

I knew that my rudimentary, pre-school Greek would never stand up to the legal jargon of the High Court and begged forgiveness for my inadequate linguistic ability. Mercifully Stathis was then allowed and sworn in as my translator.

Twitters from the audience at my lingual faux pas and confusion between translators, the bench and myself in a mixture of two languages gave the proceedings an air of surrealism.

My imagination leads me to believe that until the middle beak inquired as to what my current occupation was, the verdict had hung in the balance. The deficit in bureaucratic coffers held large sway.

I addressed the bench explaining that the Mayor of Hydra and I were working in close contact to promote tourism for the island over the Internet. Hopefully implying that I was of more value to the county as a free man.

The three then conferred briefly behind raised folders.

"Innocent, acquitted, not guilty," my lawyer simultaneously confirmed.

Absent party to cover all costs to the State.

With a bow and an "*efgaristo poli*," I walked.

And then went to get that haircut I had planned before going to court.

Like I said just about everything in this country is prone to its own sense of timing!

But better late than—

Property Pirates

Patience and timing are essential ingredients when dealing in all matters of home ownership on the island. Laws that that can be threaded back to the days of the philosophers, still influence the right to land in Greece. Two millennia of red tape!

A couple of meaningless splashes of white paint on a rock may not mean much to the average hiker but to the inhabitants, they represent a geological chess game.

The ownership of land is disputed down to the pebble.

A classic case of brinkmanship was demonstrated over a few square meters of vacant land a few of years back. A fellow, who had recently completed building three villas on a plot of land overlooking the harbour, was keen to expand his enterprise. One he day paced out a couple of meters from his boundary wall and dropped a splash of *asvesti* (white wash) on a pair of rocks, then left them for a year.

The following year he freshened the fading asvesti with larger dollops of white and painted a couple more to add definition to the perimeter.

Another year a slit trench was dug, the following, actual foundations were excavated.

Next season the concrete foundation was laid, a year later a meter of stonework masoned.

As the final roof tile went in place there was a knock on the new front door.

"*Kalimera*, thank you for building me a beautiful little house on my land and here are my papers," said the owner of the land.

Eleven years to complete the house on supposed uncontested land. Keys were handed over!

If only the pirate had waited twelve years the occupational and squatting rules would have been different.

One would think, too, that biding one's time would cement the right deal on a house.

Peter the Painter had spent nearly a decade looking for the right little spitaki to buy. Knowing the island as well as he did, he knew that decisions over property were not to be rushed and to be patient until the "right" buy came along—it did.

A "renovators dream", realistically translated means, "start-from-scratch ruin". The intended property was within the artist's budget and if he put his creative juices to work, along with some hard labour, he could put together a comfortable little cottage.

Peter, well known and well liked on the island, was rarely associated with detrimental gossip. Until that is, he shook hands on the purchase of his long searched for spitaki.

"I've never had so many people shout at me," said Pedro, looking distressed the next morning. "Wherever I went people I've known for years and liked, were coming up and giving me stick—all of them claimed a sixteenth share in the ownership of my intended purchase."

The lesson of course, is to check the paperwork.

The last will and testament sometimes contains partial "bequeathment" of an ecclesiastical nature. A gesture to the beards and Almighty at a time when these things are a sound investment, can throw a spanner into the documentation of transfer.

Then there are the curved balls, just when you think it's over the plate.

"I sold it yesterday, I didn't think you were serious and anyway they might not like it." The prospective buyers, jet lagged, looked in disbelief; newlyweds who had honeymooned in the apartment below that summer and had come a long way to do the deal.

"But Christo, we told you these people were flying all they way in from Singapore and that they had seen the place and were coming to sign."

I had given the potential buyers an honest description. They knew the location and had seen photographs on the website. We had arranged a price even, indeed were well beyond first option stuff.

However, an upholstered cash wallet had hi-jacked the deal the day before.

A shrug and an apology *tea-na-khanamay*, (what can we do), was all we got.

Indeed, the young couple took this to be a negative start and gave up on the island holiday-home idea altogether.

An elderly Dutchman, who was helping clear out his daughter's garden and the neighbourhood *platia* (empty quad) outside her front door, decided he would burn the excess rubbish. The fact that he was wearing a woollen jumper and jeans did nothing to deter a local moustache with a hose.

"I don't know what I've done but they're very excited," said Hans, dripping in the doorway.

We investigated the ruckus.

It turned out that the *platia* was in much dispute, with several parties, including the municipality in contention for its rightful ownership. The pending result had been lingering for years on a judicial desk somewhere.

Labour of any kind upon this type of land can be misconstrued as staking a claim. This apparently included the raking and burning of leaves. Hence the hose! Of course, a couple of the adjacent black shawls had emerged to verify land "jumpmanship" as well.

"Not even the *Demos* (municipality)," wagged a finger. Which would account for the lack of care.

It is by experience that one learns to ask the right questions and ignore the "right" answers.

There are a lot of right answers depending on who answers and what century of law is being employed.

The trick is to collect as many answers as possible and go with the majority.

Rats and Rhubarbs

"A toilet book!" Her first reaction didn't reflect my enthusiasm.

"Why not, there are books for the kitchen, books for the coffee table—all rooms except the loo. It's one place where some people manage to enjoy a little peace and quiet."

Kelsey, my wife who I fondly refer to as "Herself", gave me a familiar look of incredulity, so I contemplated other marketing avenues. Perhaps that was taking modesty a modicum too far, submitting one's first book at toilet level might be a little too unconventional.

Weeks later, whilst doing a preliminary scout through the PC's accumulated image files, I accidentally double-clicked on an old icon. Up popped one of the rhubarb characters—in the loo.

I took this to be a serendipitous nudge; the book was after all about life out of the rat race.

"It's as quirky as the script," I said, showing Herself my draft cover idea. "And certainly eye-catching, in keeping with the books eccentricity, don't you think?"

Whilst not relishing a reminder of the event, she conceded I had a point. A logic of sorts.

The most dangerous thing in the island's ecosystem is probably the *serranda-pothi* (centipede).

Tarantulas are a debatable second, no longer a worry to me as I now live on a different hill and semi-poisonous vipers come in a distant third in terms of potential causality risk.

One evening Herself went into the bathroom and let out a scream.

Convinced a megalo serranda-pothi could be the only possible wild life to cause such panic, I grabbed a slipper.

Whilst we are not high on its menu, these forty legged, red-brown creatures pack a sting and were at very least to be evicted from the premises. I have seen one so big it couldn't fit down a shower drain, about sixteen inches!

I bumped into the highly agitated other-half fleeing the loo, making much noise and gesturing with her hands, fisherman-tale-like, a three-foot something; the grand daddy of all centipedes I assumed.

"A giant sewer rat."

"What, where?"

"Climbing out of the toilet!"

I looked at my flimsy slipper; even if she was only half exaggerating, I was poorly armed and so headed for the kitchen to find a broom.

"It was standing with its back legs on the back of the bowl—straddled across, front paws on the lip, about to get out. It was black and wet—Imagine if I was sitting down, it was so big it could barely turn around to escape back down the pipe!" she gushed.

Later, still excited about this event, she proceeded to chastise me for *not* getting noisy about the issue as well.

"And you think it's funny!"

I explained about the need to change armaments, hence my apparent desertion from the front line.

"If indeed there was a man-eating rodent in our loo, then obviously a feather-weight, synthetic slipper wasn't going to do the job."

"What if it comes back?"

"We keep the lid down until the hardware store opens." A trap seemed the obvious solution, if only for peace of mind.

"But it can lift the lid."

"Then we'll put a weight on it."

"But what if the kid wants to use the loo in the middle of the night?"

Convinced the rat could return and finding the battening solution wanting, she resorted to defensive tactics common to many housewives. The use of chemical warfare!

A large rat was a formidable foe and Baygon wasn't going to do the trick so she went to the supermarket before it closed.

"I'll make sure he doesn't fancy coming up in my loo again," she muttered as she disappeared straight into the bathroom upon return.

The next thing I heard was the most dreadful hacking. Herself came stumbling out, gasping between coughs.

"I should have known better," she spluttered. "I did chemistry at school."

Three bottles of toxic, hydrochloric acid, topped up with lashings of chlorine based bleach. A gas to topple horses!

Wafts of noxious vapour had followed her into the living room; doors and windows flew open. Newly polished, brass door handles oxidised green.

Next morning it didn't take much sleuthing to find the cause of this rodent invasion.

"Our neighbour Jani," tutted Dina our landlady, hands on hips. He had been cleaning out his drums and had poured *petrelio* (petrol) into the communal *vothros* (septic tank). Fumes in the rat's nest had forced an evacuation. The evidence was reinforced the day after by the floating body of a juvenile rat in my bunker loo.

The neighbourhood smelled less flammable after a couple of days and I guess the surviving rats went back underground.

Jani has promised not to rinse into the vothros next spring and we now, more actively, encourage the local cat population.

Our other neighbour's cat had half a dozen kittens, which were carried off one night to a distant neighbourhood once weaned.

The sprog, my animal loving, pre-teenage step-daughter Harriet, brought them all back under cover of dark the next evening.

The neighbour's wife was looking perplexed the following morning, so Harriet decided to help her out.

"No matter where you take them, the mother is clever and will bring them home," she explained. She knew that the murder of animals is something most Greeks abhor and that now the returned kittens would at least be fed.

That was a few kitty seasons ago, so we have a lot of cats in our district these days.

No doubt, some vets will be called in soon to curtail the population; the anti-neutering lobby will complain; others will look for the paperwork; debate will ensue; somebody will think of forming a society; some may write to the papers—and rhubarbs on the rock will continue.

The alternative to the rat race is, in my experience—a rat maze. It's not speed that counts, it's how you get there; and neither way is simple.

APPENDIX

For the occasion of my 39th birthday, fellow expat, Roger Green, wrote this poem. Much to my embarrassment, he read it, at a gathering held in my honour (any excuse for a party would do) to friends at the "Pyrofani" a much-favoured restaurant. I've included it, as an example of how my "careers" on Hydra, have given amusement to others!

The Thirty-Ninth Psalm of David

Oh David,
Just a minute, please.
The Gore-Booths want some extra keys
For several guests from overseas;
And can you meet them from the Dolphin
And arrange for them to get some golf in?

Er David,
Leonard Cohen begs your pardon,
But can you tidy up his garden
And paint his house before next week?
(He wants to let it to a Greek
Who has been seriously depressed
And now requires a total rest.)
He hopes your skilled clearing up
Will speed the fellow's cheering up;
Only, he says, the truly jolly
Can give rein to their melancholy.

And David,
Brian and Julie called
To say they were appalled
To hear you haven't tiled their floors
Or washed their walls or cleaned their doors;
Less in anger than in sorrow,
They want it all done by tomorrow.

Oh David,
Jacques and Dominique
Are coming with a crew next week
(They don't know when they'll be arriving)
To make a film about pearl-diving;

117

(Yes, you heard right—not sponges,
pearls—
They need a dozen sexy girls)
Directed by Dmitri De Clerq
(He's sure he can make it work),
Set on a Caribbean shore,
So please can you lay in a store
Of shoe-polish? With you as back-up
He plans to have the Hydrans black
up.

Er David,
News from Michael Lawrence—
He bumped into Le Goff in Flo-
rence;
After some drinks the pair decided
Nevermore to be divided,
And planned a show of Art for All
In the Melina Mecouri Hall.

But David,
They need your assistance,
They're doing this thing from long
distance,
So can you undertake it all
And take ten crates round to the
Hall;
Arrange in judicious mixture
Every sculpture, every picture.
Money? No problem. Now you pay,
But you'll be reimbursed one day.
The task itself is pure simplicity.
You organise advance publicity—
Their working title strikes a balance
Between their slightly kinky talents:
They want to call it—a joke quite

harmless—
Views of Greece by Legless and
Armless

And David,
Please don't lose your temper,
But Kostis' bitch has caught distem-
per;
He fears the creature may be dying,
So will you kindly catch a flying—
Convey the doggie to the vet,
He'll be forever in your debt.
And could you pick up, while you're
there,
All the school textbooks for next
year?

Oh David,
A bewildered female
Wants you to help her with her e-
mail.

Er David,
Richard Branson needs you soon
To hold the string of his balloon.

And David,
Can you bring a donkey
To fetch a telly that's gone wonky?

Oh David,
How long will it take
To round up Gabriella's snake?

Er David,
Can you mend a light,
Unblock a loo, and book a flight?

And David,
An Israeli lawyer
Has been making inquires for yer.

But David,
Tonight you can relax,
Unplug the phone, switch off the fax,
Watch some television, soppy
Enough to make your hard disk
floppy.
On this your birthday, we wish you
well,

And everyone else can go to—Spetses,
Ermioni,   Poros—anywhere   but
Hydra.

But David,
Think how life would crawl
If nobody wanted you at all—

Written By Roger Green.
© Studio Viriditas Productions 1997

0-595-30246-7

CPSIA information can be obtained
at www.ICGtesting.com
Printed in the USA
FSOW02n0000250416
19627FS